a **Wing** and a **Prayer**

a Wing
and a
Prayer

Paul Hostetler

To Ruth —
God's best to you !
Paul

Evangel
Press

2000 Evangel Way
Nappanee, Indiana 46550-0189

Portions of this book were first published as articles in the *Evangelical Visitor* (Evangel Publishing House, Nappanee, IN 46550): "My Friends, The Amish" (Feb. 10, 1979); "The Two Cemeteries" (July 25, 1980); "Silver Nitrate, or Vitamin C, or God?" (April 10, 1974); "The Tumbleweed Caper"–first story in the chapter (June 1984); "...then the letting go..."–first portion of the chapter (April 25, 1981); "The Man We Shouldn't Have Asked"–first story in the chapter (November 1984); "Another 'Littlest Angel'" (Feb. 25, 1976); "Eighties the Best Ever!" (July 1987). Two articles were published in *Christian Living* (Mennonite Publishing House, Scottdale, PA 15683): "Kristy," (July 1987); and "The Tumbleweed Caper"–the first story in the chapter (July 1990).

Cover design: Weston Phipps

Chapter illustrations: Karen Deyhle

Library of Congress Catalog Card Number: 92-75502
ISBN: 0-916035-58-1

Printed in the United States of America

4 3 2 1

Contents

Introduction

Fifteen years went by after my father died before I got around to writing *Preacher on Wheels*, the story of his life. My intention was to write a similar book in a year or two. But alas, too many additional years have elapsed.

This book takes up, more or less, where the other left off. It relates selected incidents and observations from my own experiences, often in a family setting.

Being good parents is not easy. One reason is that each child has full freedom of choice. It follows then that even when parents fulfill their responsibilities well, their children may choose a disappointing way of life. Regardless of the circumstances, family times together can often be fun times. They should include occasions of good, clean humor and lots of hearty laughter. Family experiences, however, hold both happiness and heartbreak. Life is like that; we sometimes laugh and cry in close sequence, or even simultaneously.

Some of these chapters can be used for read-aloud times with family and friends. It worked out that way with *Preacher on Wheels*, and I hope it will be the same with this book.

You may have a question about the book title. In World War II a shell-shot bomber staggered back to its home base, barely reaching the runway. Someone said, "It's comin' in on a wing and a prayer." A song writer set the words to music, and the ballad became a hit. Family and personal crises can be described by the words of the song, with one wing being our own efforts, and the second wing representing God's good help as we pray, sometimes in desperation. Our children call the latter petitions "panic prayers."

You may also wonder if I am related to Jeff Hostetler, the well-known football quarterback. Many have questioned me on this in recent years. Jeff and I are distant cousins. He was born in Somerset County, Pennsylvania. We are both descendants of Jacob Hochstetler, who came to Pennsylvania from Switzerland in 1737.

I wish to express appreciation to the people who have, in various ways, contributed to the creation of these pages. First, to my wife Lela. She has been helpful, kind, and gracious. As I wrote this introduction in our bedroom, she was trying to sleep (5:15 a.m.) while I was clicking away at the keyboard of my laptop computer—we were with friends in Alberta, Canada. Second, to our daughters, their spouses, their children, and my sisters and brothers. They have been good critics, urging me to delete some stories ("too boring") and giving me replacements ("much more interesting"). My thanks also to Dr. E. Morris Sider, for his advice and encouragement; to Ellie Yoder, Beth Mark, Esther Ebersole, and Winnie Swalm, for reviewing the manuscript; to Karen Deyhle, for her artwork used for chapter headings (she insisted that I point out she is very much an amateur); and to Mike Huffnagle, for his technical assistance with my computer. And finally, to still others, too numerous to mention, who have made my life a better journey. The interest, involvement, and suggestions of all are treasured.

I am also grateful to the editors of *Christian Living*, Scottdale, Pennsylvania, and the *Evangelical Visitor*, Nappanee, Indiana, for permission to reprint a number of articles, or revisions of articles, published in their magazines.

In conclusion, I thank the readers of *Preacher on Wheels* who gave me words of affirmation or constructive criticism, either in person or by letter. After one man read the book, he told me "…a person doesn't need to think when reading it." I've been trying to figure out ever since whether his comment was a compliment or a complaint!

. . . Paul Hostetler

To Lela,
the First Lady of my life
"The highest gift and favor of God
is a pious, kind, godly... wife."
—Martin Luther

Chapter 1

A Wing and a Prayer

Dad and his brothers longed for more freedom and speed than carriage wheels could provide, so they began using automobiles. The same spirit of adventure prompted Dad's children to become involved in flying. Who knows?—perhaps our children dream of—or even plan for—space travel!

Of my brothers and sisters, Lloyd made the first attempt to fly. One day when he was 15 he learned about a partly assembled, home-built small airplane which was for sale for $25. Without waiting long, he bought it and, soon after, had it hauled home. Dad and Mother were a bit displeased, to state it mildly, but they were comforted by the fact that the plane was in pieces and didn't even have a motor.

But Lloyd went to work on that. He bought a small Ford V8-60 motor, sawed off the rear housing by hand (a very difficult job), mounted the engine on the front of the fuselage, and bolted a piece of 2x4 wood, about five feet long, on the flywheel in order to have something resembling a propeller. He then crawled into the open cockpit, had someone start the engine by spinning the 2x4 "propeller," revved up the motor, and imagined he was flying!

The wings were only in the framework stage, so he and another brother, Eli Jr., laboriously covered them with muslin and then saturated the muslin with dope (Lloyd's words) to tighten and strengthen the fabric.

When asked just how he was planning to fly the plane, Lloyd said he'd get it into the pasture field behind our house and fly it by degrees. His intention was to fly only a few feet from the ground until he "got the feel of the thing," and then venture ever higher. Dad was not impressed—at least not in any positive way. He had visions of Lloyd and the plane scattered in fragments on the ground as the result of a crash landing. He determined to take action.

At that point in the eager young flyer's progress, Dad sponsored a revival meeting in a large tent pitched near our house. Lloyd went forward to pray and dedicated his life to the Lord. Dad afterwards questioned him about his full consecration, and Lloyd assured him that he was God's man, no matter what. According to Lloyd, Dad read more into that statement than was ever intended.

Not many days later Dad told him he would need to sell the airplane. Lloyd was distressed, but Dad had the final word. The plane was advertised and sold—bringing a small profit. Lloyd then resolved to get himself into the sky in a more legitimate way by taking flying lessons at the small airport near Massillon, Ohio.

About a year later Lloyd took two flying lessons in a Piper Cub. He occupied the rear seat of the tandem aircraft, and the instructor, up front, obstructed his view of the instruments. Lloyd objected to this arrangement, but the instructor said he didn't need the instruments at that stage in his training.

During both lessons the instructor put the plane through various maneuvers, and it "rolled and pitched like a ship in a storm." Lloyd got sick each time, but he determined to keep flying nevertheless.

Other circumstances, however, brought an end to the lessons. He left Ohio that fall to attend Messiah College, a small Christian high school and junior college near Harrisburg, Pennsylvania. He met and became a close friend of Rupert Turman, a student from the hills of Virginia. The following summer Lloyd was invited to preach for a series of revival meetings in Rupert's home church.

One warm Saturday evening Rupert took him to a local airport to watch the airplanes. While there, Lloyd saw a small Taylorcraft which was for sale. The owner urgently needed money. "I'll sell you this airplane at the bottom dollar!"

"How much money would you take?" asked Lloyd.

"I'll let this beautiful plane go for $1,250, but only if you have the cash today."

"Sorry, fellow, I'm from Ohio and I don't have that kind of money with me." (He didn't have it anywhere else, either.)

"Well, let me see," he drawled. "I might give you a couple of days to get the money together. In the meantime, let me take you for a ride."

They climbed into the cockpit and were soon up and away. The plane was different from the Piper Cub Lloyd had used for his two lessons a year earlier. It had side-by-side seating with clear vision through the windshield, and it had a control wheel rather than a stick.

When they returned to the field Rupert called him aside. "If you want to buy that airplane, I'll lend you the money," he offered with a grin.

Lloyd was stunned. Looking longingly at the little plane, he sensed an opportunity that was too good to let pass. He shot out his hand to shake on the agreement.

According to Lloyd, "I really didn't know where the money would come from since I had none at home. But that problem could be solved later. I would get the money somehow. Dad would help if all other efforts failed," he reasoned.

Rupert pulled out his pen and wrote a check to cover the full amount. By that time it was too dark to fly again. They drove back to Rupert's home in high excitement!

As you can imagine, dreams of flying his very own airplane robbed Lloyd of sleep most of the night. At 4:00 a.m. he could stay in bed no longer. It was Sunday morning and he wanted to fly before going to Sunday School and the worship service. He dressed and drove over to Rupert's house.

Rupert was less enthusiastic but he obliged and prepared breakfast. Then they were off to the airport. Walking along the rows of airplanes, they came to the cream-colored plane with blue stripes. Lloyd climbed into the cockpit to look things over. Remember, he had received only two hours of lessons, in a different make of aircraft, and had never flown a plane alone in his life.

He asked Rupert to crank the propeller. The engine responded with the very first attempt. Rupert pulled his long, slender frame into the cramped cockpit.

"What's this dial here?" he asked, pointing to an instrument beyond the control wheel.

Lloyd shrugged his shoulders.

"Why is that needle swinging so erratically?" he persisted.

"I really don't know," Lloyd admitted. "But don't worry; I learned to fly without them."

"Well, O.K. then, let's get this plane moving."

Relieved, Lloyd taxied the plane into position at the end of the runway. Nervously he advanced the throttle. The plane accelerated rapidly and was soon aloft. They flew smoothly through the cool morning air. After experimenting with the controls—banking, turning, and climbing—

they headed back toward the field to attempt Lloyd's very first landing.

Rupert looked around anxiously. "Where's the airport?"

"It's up ahead and a little to the left," Lloyd said, pleased that he finally had an answer for one of Rupert's questions.

"That field?" he exclaimed. "We can't land in that little patch!"

Lloyd pretended to be relaxed and confident as they flew toward the end of the grass runway. A barn and electrical wires had to be crossed before the way to the field was clear. But he had approached the obstructions too slowly. The plane responded sluggishly as Lloyd wrestled to keep it under control.

In Lloyd's own words, "We staggered over the barn and then barely cleared the wires. As the ground rushed up to meet us I pulled the control wheel into my stomach. At the instant of impact the plane veered to the left, threatening a ground loop. I jammed my foot on the right rudder and pulled hard right on the control wheel."

They bounced across the runway and into a weed patch, where they stopped abruptly. It was indeed "a wing and a prayer" landing.

Without a word Rupert extracted his tall frame from the cockpit and walked away. Lloyd sat for a moment, pondering his next move. Not one to be easily discouraged, he decided to try it again, this time by himself.

Upon getting near the end of the runway, he paused to reconsider. Rupert and he had missed crashing by a very narrow margin. On the other hand, he reasoned, the first landing was fairly excusable. A few more landings should result in definite improvement.

He taxied out on the runway. As he was reaching to advance the throttle, he noticed someone running toward him, obstructing the take-off. It was Rupert, and he was swinging his arms wildly.

"Wait for me," he shouted, "I'm going along!" Breathlessly he opened the door and clambered aboard. Now there were two daring—perhaps a bit foolhardy—men in that plane!

The take-off was normal, and Lloyd's confidence returned. They relaxed and enjoyed the beautiful Virginia countryside. All too soon it was time to get back on the ground in order to arrive at the church on time.

With more caution, Lloyd returned to the field and lined up with the runway—this time at a higher altitude. But on this approach he was much too high. He pushed the plane into a steep glide, picking up excessive speed. The barn and wires whizzed by below as he leveled out over the runway.

As the far end of the runway rushed toward them, Rupert twitched in his seat. "We're going to crash!" he shouted.

Lloyd eased the wheel back, opened the throttle, and climbed to a safe altitude. He then circled the field once again and approached the runway, this time at a better, lower level, and at a slower speed.

But in spite of that, Rupert panicked. "You're going too fast; slow this thing down," he yelled.

Although Lloyd was fairly sure he was coming in just right, he pulled back on the throttle. Almost immediately, the plane lost proper gliding speed (pilots call it stalling) and refused to respond to the controls.

Lloyd's last instructor had showed him how to recover from a stall—get the nose of the plane down and open the throttle. And so, even though he was too near the ground for this, he did it.

Rupert braced himself with both hands propped against the instrument panel. Since the broad side of the barn made a straight-ahead recovery impossible, Lloyd banked the plane to the left, gritted his teeth, and waited for the plane to respond. The nose came up but the left wing would not.

"We would have made it," says Lloyd, "had it not been for a light pole next to the barnyard gate."

The left wing came within inches of clearing that final obstruction. The wrenching impact whipped the plane into a flat spin, slowing the crippled bird's fall to earth. In a billow of dust the beautiful Taylorcraft hit the ground with a jarring crunch.

"You O.K., Rupert?" Lloyd asked weakly as the dust began to settle.

"Sure, I'm all right. Let's get out of here."

Lloyd's door was jammed so they both crawled out the right door. They walked around the plane to assess the damage. The landing gear was smashed, the left wing was crumpled, and various parts of the fuselage were badly buckled.

Rupert and Lloyd soon left and went to church. Rupert didn't mention the incident to anyone, but Lloyd told the congregation the whole story before he preached the sermon. They stared in utter disbelief.

Following the service that evening, Lloyd headed back to Ohio after arranging with Rupert to send him money as soon as possible.

At home, no one had heard about the accident. Nor did Lloyd volunteer any information.

About a week later Lloyd received a phone call from Rupert. His heart began to pound as he stammered through the conversation, ending with a promise to send money the next day. When he hung up, he turned to face several pairs of questioning eyes. And so Lloyd reluctantly told the family the story of the foolish flight.

"For pity sakes," Dad began, "you could have killed yourself, and Rupert too."

Lloyd looked at the floor, hoping that Dad somehow would have a solution to the money problem. After a while Dad said, "We'll talk about it in the morning."

The next morning it was agreed that Dad would borrow the needed money so that a check could be sent to Rupert. Lloyd worked for a long time to repay the loan from the bank. Paying for a dead plane—it had been damaged beyond repair—was bitter medicine indeed (if metaphors may be mixed).

That did not, however, end the consequences of his Sunday morning flight. The Civilian Aircraft Administration (CAA) fined Lloyd a thousand dollars for operating an airplane without a pilot's license. Dad made a strong plea to the officials, and they surprisingly accepted fifty dollars and Lloyd's promise not to fly again until he had valid certification.

Several years later Rupert came to Ohio to preach in a revival meeting. Lloyd went to hear him. After the service he jokingly invited Rupert to go for an airplane ride. To his surprise, Rupert accepted without hesitation.

When they climbed into the plane, Rupert asked, "What's this instrument—or don't you know yet?" Lloyd, by then a pilot with many hours of flying, chuckled to himself as they climbed into the sky. And so they had come full circle, and both were still daring—perhaps even a bit foolhardy!

Some years later Lloyd purchased land along State Route 93 a few miles north of the Lincoln Highway (U.S. 30) and bulldozed out a landing strip for his "airport." He and others flew from it regularly.

One summer during camp meeting time at West Milton (near Dayton), he flew his small plane to the camp, landing in a field adjoining the grounds. He gave rides to venturous camp attenders, without incident even though the field was very small.

When the meetings at the camp ended, he offered to take our Uncle John Helmuth back home to Lloyd's little airport. Uncle John reluctantly agreed. As many people waved goodbye, the two men flew out of the small field the final time. Their flight home was uneventful except that Lloyd somehow lost his way—probably following the wrong road or railroad.

By the time he discovered his mistake, the sun was sinking, all too fast, in the west. Making some calculations after he finally figured out where he was (having flown too far west in a course which should have been roughly north-easterly), Lloyd realized that he would need to make an emergency landing in a farmer's field.

As all of this was going on, Uncle John, who could get very excited when receiving the proper stimulation, was becoming more and more agitated!

Lloyd looked around for a field, without any success at first. Finally, in desperation because daylight was fast fleeing, he spotted a small field (far too small in Uncle John's estimation) and made "a wing and a prayer" landing.

Uncle John climbed out of the plane with difficulty. When he got his feet on the ground, his knees were shaking so much he could barely stand up. He staggered a few steps away from the plane and then paused, turned toward Lloyd, raised his hand toward heaven, and declared, "I promise you, and God, that I will never fly in a small airplane again!"

And he kept his word.

Chapter 2

More Flying Days

In the years which followed, Lloyd twice flew to our home in Clarence Center, New York, near Buffalo. The first time he came for Rally Day in our Sunday School. He landed in a small field near the church. We wheeled the plane from there to the lawn at the street.

Our reason: we promised a free ride to anyone who brought a visitor to Sunday School. People who drove by slowed down, stopped, and even backed up—to be sure they were seeing what they *thought* they were seeing!

By Sunday noon Lloyd decided that because of wind direction it would be unsafe to take people for rides from the field he had landed in. But he still had to get the plane from that field. His plane had tandem seating, with the passenger in the seat behind the pilot. For convenience, Lloyd had taken the control stick out of the rear area (the sticks were usually in front of both seats because when alone the pilot always flew from the back seat for proper balance of the plane). And so he had a dilemma: he needed to have the plane as light as possible to help him gain altitude rapidly; yet he needed someone in the back seat for proper balance.

He explained the situation to me carefully, and wondered if I would be willing to be the passenger. It was a hard decision, but I agreed.

We got into the plane and strapped ourselves in—very carefully on my part. Lloyd taxied to the far end of the field and studied the situation. He decided he needed more field length, so he taxied to the corner of the field. He then raced the motor and started out parallel with the end of the field for about two-thirds of its width and then made a sharp left turn to line up with the direction of takeoff.

My heart was thumping as we gained speed—far too slowly, it seemed, for the length of the field. When the wheels left the ground Lloyd immediately saw that he would not gain enough altitude to clear the trees in front of us. So he banked sharply to the right. We came around in good shape until the backstop of a baseball diamond came into view—and the tip of the right wing was going straight toward it. I prayed a "panic prayer."

Just at the moment when a crash seemed certain, Lloyd brought that wingtip up. The backstop flashed under us so near I could have almost reached out and touched it! Then Lloyd immediately dropped that wing in order to complete the turn and keep us out of the nearby trees.

When we landed in a larger field, my knees, like Uncle John's of some years before, had turned to rubber. It took some real determination to stand beside the plane, appearing to have taken the whole ride in stride.

"That was a bit more difficult than I like it to be," admitted Lloyd slowly. I just nodded; my voice probably would have squeaked if I had tried to speak.

Lloyd took a large group of people for rides that afternoon, one at a time, and without incident—with one exception. We learned afterward that the flying created a problem for football fans. On every trip the plane circled the small town of Clarence Center. The fans complained that this caused distortion of incoming TV waves for an important football game.

The second time Lloyd flew to Clarence Center, he came with a four-passenger plane. He was logging cross-country miles for a requirement in his training. He called ahead of time and asked us to suggest a destination about 200 miles beyond our town. We chose my wife Lela's home town, Collingwood, Ontario.

Our three girls were small then, and Lloyd strapped the two older ones, Beth and Karen, into one rear seat, and Lela into the other seat. He, of course, had one front seat, and Helen and I had the other.

We flew over Niagara Falls and the end of Lake Ontario as we winged our way north. We landed at the field near Collingwood in grand style as Lela's family proudly watched. After our visit we flew back home again, safe and sound, to Lela's great relief. She does not share my love of flying. Our daughters thought the trip was exciting beyond description!

As I am writing this, Lloyd has just retired from his last pastorate in Salem, Oregon. All his life he dreamed of having his retirement home near an airport. Well, some dreams come true. His little home borders a small airport near New Philadelphia, Ohio. One runway is only a few steps from his back lawn.

When Lloyd and his wife Edna moved there, a friend who has a plane at that airport gave Lloyd a set of keys. "Fly the plane any time you wish," he offered. As for Lloyd, he thinks that if he isn't already in heaven, he must be camped right next to the pearly gates!

Eli Jr. (JR), who suggested changing the words "Flying Days" in the chapter title to "Flying Daze," also took flying lessons in those years, at a small, grass-strip airport near Massillon. He got his solo license on his first try at age 16.

One day he was "shooting landings." When this is done, the pilot comes in for a three-point-landing and then, just as the wheels touch the runway in what would be a good landing (or perchance a bad one!), he opens the throttle and regains altitude. He then repeats the process and comes in to shoot another landing. This is done again and again because the most difficult and dangerous part of any flight is the landing procedure.

As JR was shooting landings that day, he noticed storm clouds gathering in the west, the direction he faced as he came in for the landings. Keeping a careful eye on the clouds, he went around time after time. The wind speed and gusts came with increasing intensity, but JR naively thought this condition would afford him good landing experience in an adverse situation. In reality, he didn't have enough experience to be flying in such conditions.

On his last two take-offs, JR noticed that his flight instructor and several other men had walked out in front of the hangar and were watching him.

When he came in for what was to be an actual landing because the clouds were now much darker and closer, he saw his trainer in a car, racing toward the runway. As JR came past the car, the instructor was waving his arm frantically. JR thought something might be wrong with the plane, but feeling that he needed to come on in because of the threatening weather, he landed.

When the plane came to a stop, the trainer jumped out of his car, raced over to the plane, and jerked open the door. According to JR, "He shouted some unquotable opinions insulting my intelligence and stressing my absolute stupidity in trying to fly right into the face of a thunderstorm."

JR tried to explain that he had not planned on going around again, but he was cut off short and ordered to get the plane parked. The instructor helped him tie it down even as the storm struck, with lightning, thunder, heavy winds, and rain.

Beyond a doubt, another trip for just one more landing would have ended in disaster for the young, inexperienced pilot. From that day on JR had a new sense of respect for summer storm clouds whenever he flew near any that looked remotely threatening.

Because of other interests and responsibilities, JR did not continue flying in later years. But there is always a wistful look in his eyes when Lloyd and Virgil, our two brothers who have stayed with it much longer, are swapping stories about their air travels.

Another brother, George, also learned to fly when he was 16. He completed his instruction and passed the test for his license "with flying colors."

He continued to fly, off and on, for about five years. One day he proudly took his new bride for a ride. She hesitantly liked most everything except when he banked the plane to make turns. Joyce says, "He almost turned the airplane on its side!"

That experience probably had something to do with George's giving up flying. There were at least two other reasons. One was the lack of money to continue the "expensive hobby," and the other, says George, "was lack of motivation." For a Hostetler to say that as it relates to flying comes close to heresy!

My youngest brother, Virgil, has been flying for a long time.

One day when he was flying a single-seater, open-cockpit plane near Hershey, Pennsylvania, the engine suddenly made a loud exploding sound and instantly lost power. The entire airframe began to shake and Virg throttled back to see if the vibrations would lessen.

The lower power setting didn't help. The plane began to lose altitude. Not knowing the cause of the explosion, and fearing an engine fire, he decided to shut the motor down and go in without power because wood and fabric airplanes burn quickly. He learned afterwards that a spark plug had popped out.

Virg began looking for a place to land since he was too far from his airport. The best he could do was a farmer's corn field, with corn about a foot high. He glided the plane to "a wing and a prayer" landing among the corn rows, almost nosing it over in the soft ground.

Looking something like the Red Baron with his leather flight jacket, leather flying cap, goggles, and a white scarf, he walked toward the buildings and knocked on the front door of the farmhouse. When the elderly farmer came to the door, Virg told him he'd landed a plane in his corn field.

The farmer was totally amazed at his strange appearance. "It seemed like he stared right through me," says Virg, "to a place in aviation history I had only read about."

"But I didn't hear anything," the wizened agriculturist objected as he eyed the grounded flyer.

Virg explained that he had come down with a dead motor. "Just follow me and I'll show you my airplane."

And so the farmer followed him. When he saw the plane he became very excited—and helpful. "I'll get my tractor and pull your airplane out of my corn field," he offered. Virg accepted.

The task was accomplished even though the plane broke off some of the corn stalks. After the aircraft was sitting in the wide driveway between the house and barn, the farmer asked Virg where he was planning to take it next. "Well, I'll need to find a way to tow it back to the Hershey Airport." It was a few miles away.

The farmer immediately offered to tow the plane with his tractor, and Virg accepted. Using small, country roads, and attracting a lot of attention when people saw them, the farmer proudly towed the crippled craft back to its landing field.

When the old man was ready to return to his farm, Virg offered to pay for the damaged corn stalks and his time and effort. "No way!" declared the jovial farmer. "This is the best story I've ever had to tell my grandchildren!" Virg insisted, but the farmer waved him off, got back on his tractor, and headed happily homeward.

My guess is that he has told that story to a lot more people than just his grandchildren.

About ten years ago Virg decided to build a small airplane, totally from scratch. He got a set of plans, rolls of light sheet-aluminum, other needed supplies, and half a Volkswagen engine—cut down from the kind of motor used in the VW Beetle.

He built the little thing in his basement. And he took a large amount of good-natured ribbing about getting it out of his house. But, after more than 2,000 hours of careful work, he had the last laugh.

It is a beautiful little airplane, gleaming throughout with its polished aluminum. I saw him flying it one day, and it didn't seem possible that so small a plane could lift him off the ground.

He still has the tiny aircraft, having exhibited it at the big airshow in Oshkosh, Wisconsin. Unfortunately, he can't take me for a ride; it would never get off the ground!

In the providence of God, it has never been my privilege to take a flying lesson. I regret that very, very much. However, I have logged many air miles in my travels for the church. All of those trips have been routine, with two exceptions.

I had often wondered how I'd feel when faced with almost certain death. It happened to me one day when I was in a flight to Louisville, Kentucky. As we began to lose altitude in our long approach to the airport, I began to have an excruciating ache in my head. The pain was so intense I decided that I was having a brain hemorrhage. That seemed like a reasonable diagnosis because my father died with one.

As I struggled with the pain and the idea of death, I felt at peace with God. My life had been a good, satisfying journey, and I very much wanted to stay alive, but I also looked forward to a new kind of existence with my Lord.

Well, I didn't die. My problem was sinus congestion

which resulted in searing pain as the increasing air pressure caused by losing altitude brought about swelling in my sinus cavities. The swelling caused more pressure, and that in turn caused even more swelling and discomfort.

The pain persisted well into the night after I had gone to bed. At times it was so vicious that I would sit right up. My sinuses were sore, and bleeding slowly, for more than a week afterwards.

It was a most harrowing experience, but death has not been as foreboding an enemy since that day.

About a year after the above scare, I was flying home to the Harrisburg International Airport from Dallas. As we were approaching the airport the pilot suddenly put the aircraft into a steep dive, pulling us tightly against our seatbelts and throwing a few loose items against the cabin ceiling.

I had a window seat, and when I looked out I was looking down the chimneys of Harrisburg houses, and they were getting closer alarmingly fast!

In my commercial flights here and there, my wife and I always had an argument about flight insurance. I had statistics to prove that I was much more likely to be killed in an accident on my way to the airport than at any point in the flight. But, to give her comfort, I would always buy flight insurance.

And so as I was peering down the chimneys for those few long moments, my first thought was that after all our arguments, Lela is going to be proven right, and she will collect the insurance. As I often told her facetiously, I was worth more to her dead than alive!

The pilot quickly got the plane back on a level course and then came on the intercom system. "A small airplane strayed into our flight path," he informed us, "and I thought it best not to hit him." "Thank you, Lord," I thought, "and thank you for an alert pilot."

The pilot, however, had hardly finished speaking when he banked the craft sharply to the left. Remembering what he had just told us, I looked out my window (on the right side of the plane) and saw another small airplane flash by!

I learned later that in our maneuver to avoid hitting the first little plane, we moved into the approach pattern for small craft going into another area airport. This time our big plane was in the wrong place.

Well, our pilot finally took us on in to the airport and we landed safely. When we stopped at the unloading ramp, the lady sitting beside me wasn't able to stand to her feet. I waited a little while, and then asked if I could assist her. She just sat there, shaking and pale.

A flight attendant came and helped her. As people filed down the aisle and out of the plane, hardly anyone said a thing.

Being well acquainted with the city desk editor of the Harrisburg *Evening News*, I called him and told him my story. He said he'd print the story if he could verify it with the airline involved.

I looked for the story in the paper the next day, but it didn't appear. When I next talked to the city editor, he said that when he called the airline, they said they had no knowledge of such near misses ever happening. But to this day my brain has a deep imprint of the way chimneys look from straight up, and the way small airplanes look when they flash past the wingtip of a larger airplane.

Chapter 3

Kristy

We were in bigger trouble than we realized. Surprisingly, part of the solution came from a most unexpected source: a little pup.

Rearing a family while being involved in pastoral ministries in a local congregation can create serious conflicts between parents and children. This happened to us.

The story begins in 1962. Our family of five was living in Toronto, Ontario. A Christian land developer had given our small congregation a large lot on the growing edge of the city. It seemed like the Lord was clearly directing our fellowship of less than 30 members to "arise and build." The construction costs were kept within reach only because church members donated large amounts of volunteer labor.

Our oldest daughter Beth was 12, Karen was 11, and

Helen, eight. All three have declared that the year we built the church was the worst in their lives. "You were hardly ever at home," they eventually told us. And they were right. My wife Lela and I spent many evenings and Saturdays of too many weeks at the church, along with other church members, raking, shoveling, carrying, pounding, and painting.

Coming out of practical, hard-working stock, we felt good about the large amount of money our work was saving. But in our case, hidden costs were being exacted; family life was greatly neglected. We became physically and emotionally drained. Tempers flared, but more often than we realized, our children simply suffered in silence.

The new church was completed in the fall of 1963. In the glow of Dedication Day and the many compliments received from neighbors and friends, Lela and I completely overlooked the lack of enthusiasm among our girls. They were not rebelling; they were just completely turned off.

We were slow learners as parents. Although we tried in the days that followed to give more attention to the needs of our daughters, the demands of congregational activities all too often infringed on family priorities.

According to our daughters, we made some progress. But they've also volunteered that the next three years were "only slightly better." It now seems clear that in those years we came very close to paying too much for our devotion to the ministries of the church. Along with creating tensions, we nearly turned our offspring away from the church and the God we loved.

In 1967 we moved into a newly-built parsonage near the church. By then Beth was 17, Karen 16, and Helen 13. Lela and I were confident the girls would be delighted because the house was beautiful and had four bedrooms. But not so. Although the new home was only a few miles away, moving would make it necessary to enroll in another school system. Our daughters objected vehemently. Ironically, they would rather have changed to a new church than to a new school.

Karen was outright rebellious. As the time came nearer for moving, she became increasingly insistent that she be allowed to commute to her old school. This would have necessitated two daily trips by car on our part, plus a special tuition charge. Our answer was a reluctant but firm No. Karen was terribly distressed. One night she and I argued until almost daybreak. I won only because I was bigger.

To conserve scarce funds, we used a trailer and a pickup truck on moving day. Cold rain came down incessantly, and many gobs of mud were tracked into the new house. The whole dreary event only drove down further our teenagers' sagging spirits. When the last damp piece of furniture had been put into place, at least one of our daughters stole away to her individual room to cry.

About a week later Lela saw a notice in the paper advertising a Boston Terrier puppy. The ad had a special appeal because dear friends of ours enjoyed their little "bulldog" so much that we dreamed of owning our own some day.

"Six weeks old, $100," the ad read. Unfortunately, there was just no way our family budget could include such an expense. My wife mentioned the puppy at our dinner table. Karen and Helen were immediately interested; Beth didn't like dogs. She had an unnatural fear of canines due to a very unpleasant encounter with a large dog when she was a small child.

"What would people think if we paid $100 for a dog, even if we could afford it?" I asked.

Helen, usually mild-mannered, was angry. "Let's for once in our lives not worry about what other people think! Our family *needs* a dog!" Some additional heated words were exchanged.

Then Lela made a truly inspired proposition. "If we get a puppy, perhaps another one because this one costs too much, will you girls promise never again to mention your bad feelings about moving?" There was a sober pause, but the vision of a cuddly doggie—in their minds a pug-nosed one—was too compelling. Although Beth had reservations, she agreed with Karen and Helen. "We will never complain about moving again," they promised.

We got into our car and drove to the proper address. What the girls didn't know was that our checking account held less than $100 and our pockets only a couple of dollars. But, I reasoned, it would be fun at least to see the little Boston Terrier.

The pup was asleep in a box in the kitchen when we arrived. The owner, Mrs. Papineau, lifted it out carefully, paused, and then (of all choices) laid it in Beth's hands. The droopy-eared little animal opened an eye about half way, licked Beth's finger with its soft, warm tongue, and then wriggled itself comfortably against her sweater and went back to sleep.

Beth was smitten beyond any hope of recovery. "Please, Daddy," she implored, "we just *must* take it home with us." I looked at my wife and the other two girls. They were on Beth's side.

But a big problem remained—money. I spoke to the lady. "As you can easily see, we would like to have the puppy, but we don't have enough money." She considered us thoughtfully (we learned afterward that she never sold a dog until she had met and studied the prospective buyer). She then looked at the little black and white creature so completely oblivious of the fact that its destiny lay in balance.

Mrs. Papineau smiled. "Since it is easy to see that Penny (her name for the pup) will be much loved, and since her markings aren't quite right for a show dog, I'll let you have her for $65." She was surprised when I still hesitated. Perhaps $65 doesn't seem like a lot of money, but in 1967 that amount was something like $200 today, and we were in a constant struggle to "make ends meet." I prayed a "panic prayer"—and accepted her kind offer.

We didn't reveal the purchase price to anyone for a long time, and we waited longest to share with our church friends. Some of them just wouldn't have understood.

We took our new pet home with an overflowing feeling of reckless joy, an experience all families should indulge in about once every five years—or perhaps more often. After animated discussion, we named her Kristy because we happened to be reading *Christy*, Catherine Marshall's best-seller novel. Besides, "Penny" didn't seem becoming for a dog which had cost 6,500 pennies!

Parents of teenage children know all too well that it is very hard to have a project which the whole family continues to be enthused about over a long period of time. That had been true in our family, but Kristy captured all of us for all her days.

One of the first things we did was place a dish of warm milk in front of Kristy. And one of the first things she did was make a puddle on the floor—a true harbinger of more to come in spite of Mrs. Papineau's assurance that the pup was housebroken. "She may make a few mistakes," she had admitted. "Few" took on a new meaning in the following months!

The first night I made her a small pen in a corner of the basement. She cried all night, and all of us heard every whimper, even though we were two stories away. The next morning, with much urging, I agreed that she would not need to sleep there again. Somehow, when Lela and I weren't looking, she graduated to the girls' bedrooms— right on their beds. I mean right under the covers!

Beyond any doubt in Kristy's thinking, from that day on, she was a human being. And non-dog-lovers who observed our treatment of her sometimes concluded that we also thought she was human. Well, after all, she had a pedigree far more impressive than our own. Here are her statistics as recorded on a Canadian Kennel Club Certificate: Kristy; Sire, Twilight Dandy Sam; Dam, My Ain Tara; Sire of Sire, Panther's Ace of Spades; Dam of Sire, Duchess Josephine; Sire of Dam, Wee Tuffy of Rae-Shell; Dam of Dam, Tairy Princess. It gives me an inferiority complex!

But all her pedigrees didn't remove our constant reminders that she was a pup. One day when I was exasperated almost to the breaking point with still another chewed-up shoe, Beth put up a sign near Kristy's food dish. It quoted Proverbs 12:10: "A righteous man cares for the needs of his animals."

In God's plan of things, puppies grow up and become dogs, and that helps preserve the sanity of their owners. And, I suspect, it also helps to lengthen the lives of some dogs.

My wife has claimed that Kristy brought our family together in a significant way. Now that is a strong statement, but if a vote were taken among us, the result would be at least four to one, perhaps even unanimous. One thing is clear, our family love and unity took a definite upturn when Kristy came to our house. Perhaps part of the change could be credited to parents who were belatedly giving more careful regard to their children's feelings and needs.

Kristy did bring much happiness to all of us in the years following. Her energy was limitless and her cheerful love of anyone and everyone was infectious. A total failure as a watchdog, she would have licked the hand of a burglar entering our house at 2:00 a.m.

She became quite a performer, with a repertoire of 14 tricks. Karen taught her, and Kristy often mastered a new trick in one evening. The rest of the family would sit by, cheering her on. Among her tricks were whispering, giving a designated person a kiss, shaking hands, dancing, and praying. Incidentally, it took the longest to teach her to "pray." Maybe that characteristic in her was totally human.

One Sunday evening when I was giving the devotional lesson at church, I was reading several short, selected writings of Dr. A. W. Tozer, the great Christian and Missionary Alliance preacher and editor. Having a bit of extra time, I decided to read another item, one that I hadn't read in my office. Well, I should have! The reading was on prayer, and Dr. Tozer was venting his writer's spleen on people who "taught their dogs to pray."

The people present who had observed Kristy's tricks (she often performed at banquets and parties) reacted in two ways. Those who liked dogs were amused; those who didn't had a sense of fiendish delight with my embarrassment. As for my daughters, who should have been whispering a prayer to God on behalf of their faltering father, they giggled without much restraint.

Once into the reading, I could do nothing but persevere to the end. Tozer didn't just give his opinion and then go on to something else; he polished off his unhappy victims with a whole paragraph of criticism and sarcasm such as only he could pen.

When we returned home, Beth had Kristy pray, making sure I was watching. "Your 'father' needs it," she assured her.

Kristy loved to travel, and she especially liked to attend our church camp with us. Camp Kahquah had two services each day during Family Camp. One evening Helen decided to take our dog to the service. Kristy settled down on her lap and soon went to sleep. Now, one of her ancestors had run into a wall and bashed his nose back almost to his eyeballs. As a result, Boston Terriers make a wide variety of snorting sounds when they sleep.

That night she was fairly quiet until the speaker made a dramatic pause. "Snort—choke—snort," went Kristy. Some people laughed right out loud, and those with better control almost popped an abdominal gasket!

The minister went on but he should have known better. After a few more well-timed vocal explosions, Helen, her face the color of a ripe tomato, got up and carried the offender to less disturbing quarters.

In her seventh year Kristy developed a pronounced limp. The veterinarian examined her and said that corrective surgery was required. When he mentioned the cost, I declared that there wasn't a dog alive worth spending that much money. But my heart didn't agree with my words. A few weeks later, after her operation, she was bounding around as lively as ever.

Five more years rolled by happily. By then our daughters were graduated from college, married, and living in their own homes. As they left the nest one by one, they seemed more upset about parting with Kristy than with Lela and me. We felt left out.

After the third wedding Kristy came to our bedroom, jumped on the bed, and tried to crawl in between us. We promptly and emphatically ejected her. She stood on the floor by our bed for a long time, giving us a reproachful look. Even though she tried to join us several times more, she finally discovered that an old dog *can* learn new tricks —that her sleeping place was in a box in the kitchen. The box had a special raised bottom, heated by a small light bulb. Her's was "a dog's life."

Kristy reached old age. One day she had a convulsion. Some days later she had another, and then they began to come more frequently. On Friday morning, the 13th of October (we are *not* superstitious), she had three successive seizures. We decided that she should be taken to the vet. I said I was too busy at the office, coward that I was. My wife asked Beth, who lived nearby, to go with her. Dr. Fager examined Kristy carefully and informed them that her condition would only get worse. Sick at heart, they agreed to have her put to sleep.

They brought her body home. When I returned from the office, they tearfully informed me that it was my job to bury her. So I carried Kristy to a row of pines near our garden and dug her grave as the gentle rain began to fall. It seemed like nature was weeping with me. I knelt and tucked in the small body and slowly covered it with soft earth.

The task was done, but I was reluctant to leave. Leaning on the shovel handle, I contemplated the miniature mound covered with pine needles and mused on the mysteries of affection between pets and people. And I thanked God for the good things that had happened during the years Kristy was a part of our family.

A few years ago, Beth found a black cast-iron Boston Terrier in a novelty store. She bought it for us as a Christmas present. She looked up a number of old pictures of Kristy and with loving care touched up the iron in the proper places, including a white spot on the left-front and right-back feet, and a slightly skewed diamond on the neck. And so "Kristy" stands alertly on our hearth, eager to bound down memory's lane with us.

A postscript: In 1972, Beth and her husband Ken Mark moved into the other part of the big double house we lived in on the campus of Messiah College, near Harrisburg, Pennsylvania. About a year later, a friend of Ken's found a pup which had been thrown into a creek in an attempt to drown it. He took it home but his wife rejected his suggestion to keep the dog because they already had a big one. So he gave the pup to Ken.

Ken brought it home, and Pokey became a part of our lives too. As far as we could tell, Pokey was part Labrador Retriever, part German Shepherd, and part who-knows-what? She was a beautiful black dog, and she and Kristy often played together. She outlived Kristy. When Pokey died, both families stood sadly by as we buried her beside Kristy.

Soon afterward Ken and Beth began looking for a replacement. They found another little Boston Terrier and brought her home. Her name is Mindy, and she is a heart-warming "reincarnation" of Kristy. And thus the cycle has started all over again.

Chapter 4

Teachers Who Touched My Life

Teachers have been a very important part of my life. Let me share a few stories about them.

My very first Sunday School teacher was Deacon Jonas. I learned later that he had a pronounced Pennsylvania Dutch accent, that he was pulled out of school at about age 11 to help on the farm, and that he had never taken a course in teaching methods.

He was the deacon of the Sippo Valley Church in northeastern Ohio for many years. Deacon Jonas, I came to know, was a very good deacon. I have also come to know that almost all deacons are good people, and that this is because they are elected by fellow members of the church—persons who know all their strengths and weaknesses.

As a small boy, I was not aware of these things; I only knew that my teacher loved children without reservation, and that he loved Jesus beyond measure.

Our class met in the "Amen Corner" of the small Sippo Church, and our teacher sat on the pulpit steps. By his side was a large David C. Cook chart depicting the central point of the Sunday School lesson. This was reproduced on small cards handed out to each of us.

I don't remember many things he told us, but I do remember that he told good stories. I can't bring back his exact words, but I have instant recall of his face as he sat there and leaned toward us. I can envision his being serious, laughing, crying, expressing fears, even showing anger—all emotions to which children respond.

As I reflected on this and related matters, I long ago came to the position that the first teachers of children in Sunday School are the most important in their lives.

One day when I was about eight years old Deacon Jonas came to our house to see Dad. When I told him Dad wasn't at home, I assumed he'd leave and come back another time. But he stayed.

He hoisted himself onto a counter-top in the hatchery part of Dad's various operations and suggested that I sit beside him. I got myself in place next to him, with some difficulty. Deacon Jonas was a big man. I was small for my age, as Mother was always informing people, to my dismay.

Deacon Jonas talked to me without condescension. We conversed about the weather, his farming, Dad's hatchery and feedmill businesses. You know—the kind of things adults talk about.

I crawled up on that counter thinking of myself as a boy; I slid off and shook hands with that good man (at his instigation) regarding myself as a grown-up. All because a true gentleman treated me as an equal. I shall never forget it!

Our family was often at his house for Sunday dinner. There were eight children in our family, and nine or ten in

Deacon Jonas' family—just the right amount for a good ball game. At times we would play before the meal. Sometimes Deacon Jonas would join us. And when he did, we could always predict what would happen.

He was a good hitter, and would hit that ball far over our heads. But he was overweight and ran "too much in the same place." As a result, he hardly ever got beyond first base on his hit.

Then came the big moment!

Everyone knew that Deacon Jonas would continue toward second base, or third, or home. Somehow we always got the ball to the proper base ahead of him. Looking back, I now know that he must have arranged to run very slowly so that we could have someone there waiting to tag him out.

My memory spans five decades. I am waiting at a base. I see a very large man charging toward me. He is huffing and puffing, and the ground is trembling. But the earth quakes as he hits the ground and slides toward me in a cloud of dust, with his foot stopping just short of the base. I slap the ball on that foot, and our whole team yells, "You're OUT! You're OUT!" as they converge around the fallen hero.

Before long "Aunt Lizzie" calls us all to dinner, and we tell her that we have gotten Deacon Jonas out once again. That wise woman only observes that if her man could run a little bit faster, he would get to the base before the ball.

It was good that we played ball before dinner because we were in poor shape to play afterwards. We were too stuffed with Aunt Lizzie's meat, mashed potatoes, dark brown gravy, and salads, plus cracker pudding and pie and cake, to mention just a few of her mouth-watering delicacies.

Dad had a dream about heaven one night. One thing he noticed was that there were many children there. If that dream was correct, and I am sure it was, children in heaven should have a slow-running uncle playing ball with them. He would try for an extra base, and he would be out every time. Then a favorite aunt would call all the excited girls and boys to a table groaning with the weight of good food.

The well-known Dr. Ernest Boyer said recently that elementary teachers should be the highest paid educators in our classrooms because they make the biggest difference in students' lives. I feel his words are particularly relevant in the early grades.

For my second and third grades, I attended the Number 10 School on the County Line Road about a mile west of North Lawrence, Ohio. It was a one-room building, and the teacher was Miss Mackey. I came to love her with all my heart.

Miss Mackey taught me how to read and really enjoy it. Each morning she stood in front of the eight grades and read from a classic children's book. We all joined her on her "magic carpet" and flew to far away places to discover Alice in Wonderland, Abraham Lincoln, Oliver Twist, King David, the Arabian Knights, Tom Sawyer, and many others.

When I eagerly responded in reading lessons, she kept getting me additional books to read on my own. (I learned a few years ago from another of my good teachers, Mary Fletcher, that Miss Mackey "begged, borrowed, and stole" books from all possible sources to keep her pupils reading. In this way she gave each of us our very own magic carpet.)

After my completion of Grade 3, our family moved to the North Lawrence school district. A few years later, when I was in the sixth grade, the Number 10 School was closed and Miss Mackey came to the North Lawrence School as the teacher of the first three grades.

I wasn't aware of this until I saw her out in the school yard one day soon after the opening of school. She was surrounded with happy, playing children. When she saw me she rushed over and gave me a big hug and kiss.

Coming from a very undemonstrative family (I never saw my father kiss my mother although it was always clear to me that they loved each other very much), her gesture both highly pleased and greatly embarrassed this 11-year-old. The boys in my class snickered and hooted.

Through the years I have kept my magic carpet and it has caught me away to numberless high adventures. I have believed and questioned. I have rejoiced and mourned. I've been stretched and I've been squashed. In time, I joined the ranks of those who help "manufacture" the carpets.

A few years ago I went back to Ohio to visit this remarkable teacher. She was an older version of my beloved Miss Mackey, but her eyes glowed with the same love and earnestness. She had been happily married for many years and was now Mrs. Amstutz. My boyish love for her caused me, even then, to feel jealous of her husband.

I told her that I was at long last getting around to thanking her for the great influence for good she had been on my life. I mentioned her care, her skills, and the passion for reading she had instilled in me more than 50 years before. We reminisced together as time stood still.

When I was on my feet, ready to leave, I reminded her of the time she embarrassed me in the school yard. I told her I was going to "embarrass" her in front of her husband. I took her in my arms and kissed her. She was in tears and I was too. Her husband smiled his approval.

More recently I called Principal Robert Horner of the Tuslaw High School on Manchester Avenue, near Massillon, Ohio. We laid plans, at my suggestion, for me to present a citation in honor of Miss Mackey, now 81 years old, at a dinner where various honors and scholarships would be presented to graduates on May 4, 1992. Both Miss Mackey and I eagerly looked forward to that evening, 60 years after she taught me.

Some weeks later, my Miss Mackey disappointed me for the first time ever. She called to tell me she had decided not to be involved in the big event after all. I urged her to reconsider, but teachers have the last word, it seems. A few days later I received a picture she had taken of me at the schoolhouse door six decades ago. Only a mother and a devoted teacher could have loved that ragtag lad.

Here's to my Miss Mackey! Three cheers for her and all other good teachers, and may God help them understand that there are many, many of us, riding about on enchanting magic carpets, forever grateful for their investment in our lives. Regrettably, most of us haven't done very well in expressing our appreciation.

One more story—about Sharon Weisser, a teacher younger than I who touched my life in a completely different way. Joe Miller was the deacon in the first church I pastored, in Clarence Center, New York. He was much interested in bringing new people to our church. One day he and his wife Trena drove out into the country north of town, knocking on doors and inviting people to church.

They came to the Weisser home. Jim and Edna Weisser were courteous but made it clear that they weren't interested in coming to church. They went on to say, however, that they'd be willing to have their two little girls, Pat and Sharon, attend our Sunday School if someone would be willing to pick them up and bring them back. Joe and Trena immediately promised to be at the door every Sunday morning.

And faithfully they did so for quite a number of years.

I can remember the girls well, bright-eyed, pig-tailed, and neatly dressed. Pat was 12, and Sharon 11. I don't recall that they ever misbehaved, but then I didn't have them in a Sunday School class!

They came regularly, accepted Christ as their Savior, were baptized, and joined the church. They completed grade school and high school, becoming an increasingly vital part of our congregational life and ministry.

In 1958 their mother, Edna, was baptized and joined the church. She became the first woman to serve on the Clarence Center Church Board. Five years later their sister Joan Cialfi began attending and continues at this writing.

After working several years at a nearby business, Pat went off to Messiah College for one year and then returned to her job. Sharon, feeling a call to overseas missions, went to the same college and received her undergraduate degree.

Sharon taught in public schools in Pennsylvania and New York, and then went to Southern Rhodesia (now Zimbabwe) to teach in a mission school. She served as a faithful, joyous missionary until the Mission Board highly recommended that all the missionaries in Zimbabwe come home because of great danger to their lives, due to the rebellion against the white government.

Sharon came home in 1978. Since that time she has taught at Shalom Christian Academy, a school in southern Pennsylvania, near Greencastle.

A few years ago, when I was serving on the program committee making plans for the biennial church-wide conference at Azusa University in California, we were selecting speakers for the theme sermons. Such messages are given before the business sessions each morning, and it has always been a high honor to be selected to speak.

Someone suggested that at least one of the assignments be given to a woman. I heartily agreed. Although a few women had served in this way before, one good brother, a general administrator who should have known better, allowed that if we had a woman serve, the whole thing might result in a disaster.

Disaster indeed! I was incensed with his insensitivity. I told him and the others at the committee meeting that there had been times in the past when male speakers had been a disaster. Total disappointments. Washouts. People went to sleep, and some who didn't probably wished they would have.

The committee decided to risk having one woman give a theme sermon. As you might surmise, I recommended Sharon Weisser. I had heard her speak only once before, at our Roxbury Camp, and she had done very well. We decided to ask her to serve.

When I talked to her about the assignment, I told her, a bit facetiously, that I had staked my reputation on her. I strongly encouraged her to accept the responsibility. Then I told her that she would receive no expense money and no honorarium. (This has been our policy for speakers from our own denomination.)

I also told her to just be herself and not let the large crowd intimidate her. She promised to do her best, but she said that her specialty was teaching, not preaching.

In due time she sent me the money for her registration fee, meals, and lodging. At the time I was serving as the denominational convention director and registrations were coming to my office. (Actually, my wife Lela did much of the work, while I got the credit—a fairly flattering arrangement!)

Not long after that I received a letter from Sharon's sister Pat. She had learned of Sharon's plans, and she told me that if I had received any money from Sharon, I was to send it back. She, Pat, would pay registration, meals, and lodging for Sharon, and she would also take Sharon from Pennsylvania to California in her own car and at her own expense.

This was not Pat's first such gesture. Our missionaries received very meager allowances from our mission board in those years—about enough to buy toothpaste and a few other things. All missionaries, Sharon included, soon learned that financial assistance from family or other friends was a necessity. And Pat filled that need in her sister's life for many years.

When Sharon gave her message at the conference, she did a superb job. She had the large crowd laughing and crying as she delivered a dramatic sermon on true worship.

She referred to me as her former pastor and said that she used to listen to my boring sermons in her childhood and teen years and dream of the day when the roles could be reversed. And now that moment had arrived! The assembly loved it!

After the session I went to Sharon, gave her a big hug, and told her how very, very proud I was of her. Many others complimented her for her stirring message. One pastor commented, "Sharon was a real pistol!"

All messages at the conference were taped and made

available to anyone interested. The tape of Sharon's message was second only to the Wednesday evening rally message given by E.V. Hill, the black California pastor of world renown.

Pat was seated far back in that huge mass of people. Hardly anyone knew she was there. She rejoiced quietly as her sister was in the limelight. She beamed when I talked to her about how well Sharon had done. I hugged her too, with just as much delight as I had her sister.

Here was a good woman who had been a devout, devoted layperson in her local congregation, serving in many important capacities for many years.

Every time I think of this story, I remember that the Bible talks of rewards and mansions which our Lord Jesus is preparing in heaven for all his faithful followers. And as I think of what he is getting ready for Pat and Sharon, I honestly don't know whose reward will be greater.

Chapter 5

My Friends, the Amish

Would you drive over 300 miles to attend a church service? In a barn? On backless benches? We did.

My father's roots were in the Old Order Amish Church in Holmes County, Ohio. In my growing-up years we often visited my grandparents, who lived on a small farm south of Mount Hope.

As an adult, I long had a hankering to return to Holmes County and attend a worship service in what was once Dad's home congregation. In the summer of 1978 I hesitantly mentioned my yearnings to the late Mary Hochstetler, a venerable cousin who lived with her niece, Lydiann (Mrs. Levi Schrock), on a farm adjoining the one where my grandparents used to live.

Mary promptly invited my wife and me to attend a

Sunday meeting on the Schrock farm in the fall. When she mentioned that a baptism and reception service would be included, we said we would try to come.

But then I thought of a possible problem. I asked Mary (never married and now well up in years) if the bishop of her congregation would need to be contacted for approval. "Ach," she assured me, "you folks chust come. I'll get the bishop's approval."

Although we lived 335 miles away, near Harrisburg, Pennsylvania, we kept our appointment, arriving about fifteen minutes before the opening time on a beautiful September morning. To our surprise everyone in the congregation of some 200 was already present. What a refreshing contrast to the last-minute rush in our own church.

Our car was a white Plymouth Volare with a red vinyl top. It was quickly obvious that the buggies were taking all the available parking space. However, a few alert young men came forward to move some of the buggies just enough that our car could be parked among them. What a contrast—all those black buggies with one white and red car among them. It just didn't seem to fit the setting.

The service was in the upper level of their large barn. A light blanket of fragrant hay covered two wide barn-floors, and backless benches were in long rows across the full width of the building. The women, seated on one barn-floor, faced the men, who were seated on the other barn-floor, with the front rows barely six feet apart.

We were given seats of honor in the second row of the women's section, just behind where seating was reserved for the ministers and applicants for membership. We had been offered more comfortable seating, but elected to sit on the benches—to our regret later in the service.

A few minutes before nine the young unmarried women filed in together and sat near the front of the women's section. Just before the service started, the single fellows came in and sat in the rear of the men's section.

Promptly on the hour one of the men announced a hymn from their German hymnbook. He then led the group, singing short lines alone from time to time. The singing was solemn and slow, and in one part only. That first hymn, like many in the book, had numerous verses and took all of twenty minutes to sing.

Soon after the congregation began singing, the people who were to be baptized and received into the church (five young women and two young men aged about 18 to 21) got up and went elsewhere for their final counseling. This, I was told later, was the last of nine such sessions during the preceding 18 weeks. (The Amish always convene for worship on alternate Sundays.)

Upon the completion of the first hymn, everyone sat in meditation for a long moment, after which the leader announced a second hymn. As the last verse was being sung, the people in the membership class returned. Following another long pause, the third hymn was called out and sung. Near its conclusion, the bishop and four other ministers came in for the first time and sat on the bench directly ahead of us.

A young preacher, John J. Yoder, then stood and gave the first sermon, a half-hour discourse. Although the hymns and Scriptures were in German, his message was in Pennsylvania Dutch and therefore comprehensible to me since in my boyhood years it was always spoken at home.

After he finished, we knelt on the hay and prayed in silence for what seemed like ten minutes. We next stood during the reading of a scripture lesson from the third chapter of John's Gospel.

Bishop Mahlon Hochstetler then gave the main sermon, a long message in which he traced the thread of salvation through both Testaments and the doctrine of baptism in the New Testament. The subject was large and important, and quite understandably occupied almost two hours.

Before he began to speak, all the single men, except those in the baptism class, went out—presumably for a break. They straggled back in at various intervals for the next thirty minutes. The young women, made of sterner stuff, remained with us older ones. Mothers were coming and going with small children after about the first hour of what is usually a three-hour service.

When Bishop Hochstetler ended his sermon, he instructed the membership applicants, who were sitting just ahead of us, to kneel facing him. He gave them a final exhortation and then proceeded with the baptisms, assisted by Adam A. Yoder, a deacon.

The ceremony was simple, dignified, beautiful. The bishop cupped his hands over the head of each applicant and intoned a ritual while the deacon poured a bit of water three times *im Namen des Vaters, und des Sohnes, und des heiligen Geistes.*

When all had been baptized, the bishop took them by the hand one at a time, raised them to their feet, and installed them as members of the church. He sealed the bond by giving the biblical holy kiss to the young fellows, while his wife gave the same greeting to the girls.

Before the closing prayer, as is the custom, each of the other four preachers made comments of appreciation and affirmation. After another hymn was sung, the service, by now more than four hours long, ended with a prayer.

Despite the discomfort of our aching backs, the meeting was a thoroughly delightful experience for us, and we shall always treasure it. Following the benediction, I chatted with the Bishop and others about our common Anabaptist heritage.

The Amish host always serves the noon meal to the entire assembly. The group was far too large for one seating, but all were served in a remarkably short time—the men in the living room of the large farmhouse, the women in the kitchen, and the younger ones in the basement. Although conversation is much easier for them in Pennsylvania Dutch, our friends seated near us courteously spoke English for our benefit.

The meal included the famous Trail Bologna (made in a nearby town, Trail), Swiss cheese, pickles, homemade bread, a tasty blending of Karo Syrup and peanut butter,

and coffee. Lydiann Schrock urged the delicious and bountiful food upon us until we were more than satisfied.

As we drove slowly away through the scenic Holmes
County hills, I meditated on many things, including the
might-have-beens. But for various circumstances, which
included my parents' moving away from the community, I
might well at that very moment be riding home from
church in an Amish buggy. And my musings included some
longings for the peaceful lifestyle of my Amish friends.

BARBARA
ZUG. WIFE OF
S. HOCHSTETLER
DIED
JULY 29, 1852
AGED
74 Y. 8 M. 18 D.

SOLOMON
HOCHSTETLER
DIED
NOV. 3, 1863
AGED
78 Y. 7 M. 18 D.

Chapter 6

The Two Cemeteries

A rural community in Ohio has two quaint cemeteries. One is tucked away on the back acreage of a farm in Holmes County, the largest Amish settlement in the world. It has only two graves.

The other burial place, a bit larger with all of two dozen headstones, is on another farm five miles away. But the symbolic distance is much greater. This is significant to me because the bodies of relatives are in both cemeteries.

In the early years of their marriage, John and Magdalene Hochstetler lived on a farm in Somerset County, Pennsylvania. Magdalene's sister, Barbara Lehman, lived with them, helping to care for their six-month-old daughter and also assisting on the farm, which included a maple sugar camp.

One spring night after supper John went back to work at the sugar camp, about 200 feet from the house. Knowing that he needed help with boiling down the maple sap, Magdalene decided to join him after she finished doing the household chores. When she noticed that baby Susanna had fallen asleep in her cradle, Magdalene suggested that Barbara go with her.

They secured the feather cover over the sleeping child with a heavy string and then hurried across the short distance to help John with his task.

When all three returned to the house a while later, the baby was gone from the cradle. The string had been broken and the coverlet turned to one side. As cold fear chilled them, they searched through every room in the house. Unsuccessful, they returned to a bedroom which had a tall bed with a trundle bed underneath.

John reached down to pull the trundle bed out, but it stuck tight. He and Magdalene then pulled up the mattress of the top bed and, to their horror, discovered Susanna. According to a later official report, "They found the child sunk down in the lower bed with the upper bed pressed down tight upon it, and it was dead."

The next day twelve men of the immediate area were called together to assist in an inquest by the local Justice of the Peace. When he filed his report, it said in part: "The said twelve good men, who respectively do say that the child was smothered dead between the upper and lower bed, but by whom it is unknown, know not whom to suspect, as there was no person in or about the house that night."

But the facts were otherwise. Upon making the shattering discovery of the little body the night before, John rushed to his neighbors for help, leaving his wife and Barbara alone in the house.

Suddenly, Barbara saw a man peering through the window. Although he stood in the shadows, she noticed he was wearing a colorful hunting shirt. In desperation she grabbed a piece of firewood, but when she turned back toward the window, the dimly-lit figure was gone.

When asked who the night visitor might have been, Barbara named John's brother Solomon, who lived nearby. The suspicion seemed to fit because Solomon did in fact have a hunting shirt which matched her description. And what is more, John and Magdalene were inclined to believe the accusation because, as sometimes happens even among godly people, they were not on speaking terms with Solomon.

Why these facts and suspicions were not reported at the inquest, no one will ever know.

Solomon didn't learn until after the funeral that he was suspected. He immediately declared his innocence, and his wife, well known in the community as a truthful person, declared that Solomon was at home the evening of the murder and never away from the house all night. In spite of this, many who knew about the tragic happening, including some relatives, believed him guilty.

The accused man then proposed a drastic "test." He demanded that the child's body be exhumed so that he could prove his innocence by touching it in the presence of all. People in those long-ago days believed that if the murderer were to touch his victim, some sign of blood would appear—some manifestation. But the child's grandfather protested, and the test was not made.

From that day on John would have nothing to do with his brother, and others began to avoid him. After enduring the unrelenting hostility for two years, Solomon and his wife moved to Holmes County, Ohio. But the accusation followed him and hung over him. He began drinking to deaden the pain of his aching heart.

Twenty-four years after that fateful night John and his family also moved to Ohio, settling about five miles from his brother's farm. Although he lived there until his death 22 years later, John was never reconciled with Solomon, always believing he had smothered little Susanna.

A few years after John died Solomon, weary in spirit

from a half century of estrangement and the resulting broken relationship with God, found a minister who helped him renew his faith. Despite the allegations against Solomon, the good Amish bishop baptized him and received him into church fellowship.

Two years later Henry Yoder, over 70 years old and living in adjoining Wayne County, became very ill. Sure that he was going to die, he called for his minister and confessed he had killed Susanna 50 years earlier, and that he had been wearing a colorful hunting shirt.

The news was speedily conveyed across the miles. Solomon wept in anguish. "If only John was living so that I could go and give him a handshake."

As for the maker of the sordid confession, he apparently felt so relieved upon getting the 50-year load of guilt off his shoulders that he recovered. At his pastor's insistence, they went to a local judge and revealed the whole, gruesome story. The judge, considering the fact that the murder was committed in another state and that almost everyone in any way connected with it was dead, advised that the matter be dropped.

Although he was never tried in court, fifty years of guilt, with full knowledge of the alienation he caused between two brothers, must surely have punished Henry Yoder severely.

Why did he do it? Well, back in Pennsylvania he was much in love with Barbara, but she did not reciprocate. John and Magdalene (Barbara's sister) were also opposed to Henry's interests.

On that spring night, so many years before, the suitor had come to court Barbara. When she and her sister hurried from the house to the sugar camp, he concluded that they were avoiding him.

In his fury he felt like striking out at something—at anything. He entered the house and vented his insane rage on innocent little Susanna. It was a vicious, evil act which haunted him for a long lifetime.

A few summers ago I decided to find the two brothers'

graves. Going first to the small family cemetery where John and Magdalene are buried among their loved ones, including my grandparents, I looked at John's old stone with a final date of 1856, and thought some long, long thoughts. I reminded myself that I have also believed people guilty without sufficient proof. It's called prejudging—prejudice is a close relative.

Then I drove over the rolling hills and among the fertile fields to find the burial place where Solomon and his wife lie alone. I knocked on the door of the farmhouse and asked to be taken to the site of the graves. Lyle Hostetler, who is a direct descendant of Solomon, kindly consented. We drove up a steep, winding lane, through a gate into a pasture field, and to the top of a high hill.

The two weathered headstones were at the very crest of the hill, overlooking a scenic valley. As far as I could tell, they were facing the other cemetery, perhaps in a gesture of longing and forgiveness.

The horses and cattle had neatly trimmed the grass around the stones. I knelt to take a picture as the western sun warmed my back and softened the rich color tones of the old sandstones. I stayed on my knees and pondered the truth that I was a blood relative of John and Solomon. And little Susanna. And the murderer. In humble meditation, I sorrowed for "man's inhumanity to man."

Chapter 7

Silver Nitrate, or Vitamin C, or God?

For almost 50 years of my life my first conscious act when I awakened in the morning was to swallow. The purpose of this habit was to see if a sore throat had moved in on me during the night hours.

In 1972, three years after we had moved to the Messiah College campus, something happened that made my morning "medical check" unnecessary, and therein lies a tale which is told to the glory of God.

Prior to 1972, sore throat mornings happened innumerable times as far back as memory serves. The pattern was usually the same. One tonsil would be inflamed first and then despite all throat swabs, sputtering gargles, and sundry medications to the contrary, the infection would move next door to the other tonsil. With luck, the whole thing cleared up in a week or so.

At least eight or ten times that I can recall, the dreaded "strep throat" would throttle me. Each time, I became very ill and had to go to bed.

The offending tonsils were never removed; my parents were slow to take such steps. In my adult years, even though a succession of doctors looked at these offending throat guardians, none ever suggested removing them. And, of course, I never proposed an encounter with a surgeon's knife!

Then, in January of 1972, the throat plague struck again. This time it seemed intent on moving in for the kill—literally. For two weeks I was more ill than ever before. In the midst of hallucinations, severe pain, and high fever, there were days when it was difficult for me to determine if I was awake or sleeping. My physical and emotional conditions deteriorated until I despaired of life itself. Trips to the doctor's office and change of antibiotics brought no relief. Swallowing was sheer torture, and done only with conscious determination.

I was praying, and others of the church were praying. One morning I asked my wife Lela to kneel down and pray a special prayer for me. She did this, and God was very near.

An hour or so later I had her look at my throat, and she was distressed to notice that the spots on my tonsils were larger than ever. So once again we headed for the doctor. He took one look and decided to resort to silver nitrate, placing it directly on the angry infections with a slender glass rod.

After getting back home I decided to discontinue taking the medications previously prescribed on the grounds that if they hadn't helped in two weeks, they probably were not about to begin.

Foolish? Perhaps. But it was "a wing and a prayer" crisis. From that time I began to recover rapidly. During those days of recovery I asked God to spare me from ever needing to suffer such pain again.

Then three interesting things happened in the course of forty-eight hours. First, I read a magazine article which stated that, according to Dr. Linus Pauling, sufficient Vitamin C would either prevent or greatly limit sore throats and colds. Next, a TV program stressed a similar diet. And finally, a friend told me that regular drinking of orange juice had helped him overcome problems like mine.

So, in February of that year I told the good Lord, and my wife, that I was going to have a large glass of orange juice each morning for the rest of my life. Then, for good measure, I decided to have another one each evening. And praise the Lord, my tonsils have been tame ever since! Each morning I drink my juice with thanksgiving.

My children feared that I had become some kind of "juice nut," as a friend in Indiana called me. My wife suspected that the silver nitrate brought the cure. I gave at least some credit to her fervent prayer at my bedside. In deference to her, a few years later I discontinued "taking the juice medicine" each evening.

My father, who died at Easter time in 1965, believed deeply in divine healing. He just loved to testify about healings in his life, his family, and many others when given the opportunity at prayer meetings, love feasts, and camp meetings.

I just wish he could have lived to tell my story. It would have been more convincing, I am sure.

Perhaps he already has told it, say to Job, as they compared notes while leaning up against a Tree of Life. His revised version would give scant attention to vitamins and juice. That's the way godly parents are, you know.

One story Dad loved to tell involved my brother Lloyd. It happened in 1945 when Lloyd was 19. World War II had just ended and Christians in North America were eager to help with rehabilitation in Europe. The Church of the Brethren initiated the "Heifer Project."

Shiploads of donated heifers were sent to war-ravaged countries. One was given to each family who had no cattle, with the agreement that the first heifer calf would be given to another poor family. That family, in turn, was obligated to do the same with their first heifer calf, and so on. It was a marvelous plan, ultimately helping many thousands of needy families.

The United Nations Relief and Rehabilitation Association (UNRRA) supplied the transportation, on the upper and lower decks of old Liberty ships. Volunteer "cowboys," provided by the participating churches, took care of the animals enroute.

Lloyd volunteered. His cousin Paul Glick also signed up. They were technically Merchant Marines, but personnel listings did not include cowboys! And so they were signed on as engine wipers. When we referred to them, we sometimes said, in the words of John the Baptist, "Oh generation of vipers," pronouncing the last word with the German "W"!

The ship sailed from Baltimore. After two weeks at sea, the livestock were unloaded at Brindizi, Italy. The next stop was Bari, Italy, and the final port before returning to the Atlantic was Cantania, Sicily.

The city was at the base of Mt. Etna, an active volcano. Since the ship was scheduled to leave in eight hours, the captain advised the cowboys to stay in the city. About a dozen of them milled around the city for a while, and then decided to get transportation to the top of the mountain.

They finally found a man with a flatbed truck with side racks. Each young man paid a small fare and climbed on board. They were unaware that the truck had been stolen and that it had poor brakes.

As they labored up the mountain in low gear, the incline became steeper and steeper. When the road ended, they climbed the remaining distance on foot. Returning to the truck a few hours later, tired and footsore, they relaxed as the truck started down the mountainside. Lloyd and Cousin Paul were seated at the tailgate.

The truck began picking up speed, and it soon became apparent that the brakes were failing. There was a loud grinding of gears as the driver attempted to shift into a lower range. He failed and the engine stalled. In seconds they were free-wheeling down the steep mountain road. Three of the boys jumped overboard, and one was instantly killed.

Alarmed, Lloyd scrambled to his feet. The truck careened crazily as it slammed against the stone walls on both sides of the road. Tires screeched, metal rattled, and the truck bed vibrated as they continued their ill-fated ride. There was time for only a "panic prayer."

Paul, his curly hair whipping about in the rush of air, was holding tightly to the tailgate. He had told Lloyd just that morning of his coming wedding, only a month away.

Lloyd turned from him to look over the cab and saw a long stretch of road leading to a sharp curve to the right. A three-foot stone wall was the only protection from a deep ravine, covered with hardened lava, hundreds of feet below. Lloyd says, "I slumped to the floor of the truck bed, put my head between my knees, and waited for the end." All too soon the loud crash came.

After some time, another truck came up the mountain. Seeing the chassis and engine of a truck crushed against the stone wall, the driver stopped. He and another man toiled for hours, retrieving the dead and injured from the ravine and placing them on their truck.

Lloyd slowly regained consciousness. His first thought was that he was still on the first truck. A Virginian who had jumped off the truck farther up the hill noticed Lloyd move. "Thank God, at least one of you is alive!" he declared fervently. Lloyd lost consciousness again.

His next memory was of white-suited men placing him on a stretcher. For the first time Lloyd was aware his condition was serious. His hip, back, and head ached excruciatingly. They wheeled him into a room where two doctors examined him. They shook their heads and left. A bit later he was taken to a dark room and placed in bed, fully clothed.

Lloyd learned later that the doctors had no hope for his

recovery. He had a broken back, crushed hip, shattered jaw, and a massive concussion. Morphine helped deaden the pain. When he cried out in agony, another needle was administered.

He learned that Paul had died in the accident. For eight days Lloyd lay on the cot, unable to move or eat. He became progressively weaker. He was at the point of death, and welcomed it.

Back home in Ohio, word had finally arrived concerning the accident. The family was stunned at the news of Lloyd's serious injuries and Paul's death. Word spread rapidly and prayers began to ascend to God for Lloyd's recovery. Dad, a great prayer warrior and believer in divine healing, interceded in faith.

The timing was crucial. The doctors felt the ninth day would be Lloyd's last. Lloyd says, "I knew death was near because I no longer felt any pain. With cold hands I felt my lifeless body. The only warm spot was around my heart."

Three American clergymen were in Rome. They heard of the accident and flew to Sicily. They walked into Lloyd's room on the fateful tenth day. They approached his bed and asked, "Would you like us to anoint you and pray for your healing?" Lloyd nodded weakly.

They removed the icepacks from around his head, anointed and prayed for him, replaced the icepacks, and left.

For the first time Lloyd sensed a will to live. Now was his time to act in faith. He removed the icepacks with great difficulty. He began to feel much better! When the nurse came into the room to give the usual shot of morphine, Lloyd refused it. "I don't need it anymore," he said in a clear voice.

The nurse turned pale. "I'm healed!" Lloyd continued. "Feel me; I'm getting warm again. I'm going to live! The Lord healed me!" A doctor soon came in and examined him. He shook his head in amazement.

It was decided to move Lloyd and the two other survivors of the accident to Naples. After arriving at the hospital there, Lloyd announced that he was very hungry. A nurse soon brought him a hamburger and a glass of orange juice. Says Lloyd, "It was the best food I had ever eaten!"

From that time on he ate regular meals in the dining room. He thanked God again and again, and the events of the past weeks began to fade. Some days later, a doctor released him from the hospital. In due time he was booked on the passenger liner *Saturnia*, headed for New York City, and on a train from that city to Massillon, Ohio.

During all those long weeks Dad and Mother had not received any direct word from Lloyd. Their only information was gleaned from the local newspaper and UNRRA. They continued in prayer.

One day there was knock on the door. When Dad answered it, "There stood Lloyd with a heavy suitcase in each hand! God had worked a mighty miracle of healing!"

Dad had had chronic heart problems for many years. It's a wonder that when he saw Lloyd he didn't have a fatal heart attack.

Chapter 8

The Tumbleweed Caper

Our daughter Beth is a good writer. A few of her published articles which follow will prove the point. I have chosen these particular ones because they involve our whole family.

The Tumbleweed Caper
by Beth Hostetler Mark

When my children ask me to take them wading in the creek, or a friend invites me to spend the afternoon shopping, I often refuse because it isn't in my plans for that day. But sometimes the "tumbleweed caper" comes to mind and, leaving unwashed dishes and laundry behind, I have a good time with my children or friend.

It happened the year I was nineteen when our family was on a camping trip to a church conference in California.

We saw many interesting sights on our way west—the Grand Canyon, Navajo Mission, the Painted Desert, and Hoover Dam, to name just a few. But our most often remembered "sight" did not even attract most tourists.

As we travelled in the southwest, my two sisters and I became intrigued with the tumbleweeds we saw dancing across the desert. Some of them got caught in the fences close to the highway. One day we talked Dad into stopping so we could see them up-close.

Once we examined them, we got the notion that they were cute and that it would be fun to take some along home, spray paint them, and hang them in our rooms. After some fast talking on our part, Dad agreed to let us keep them.

Our next problem was finding a place to put the weeds. (For those who know the tumbleweed only from the song, it is a large, round—24 to 36 inches in diameter—dry, woody, and very prickly dead plant. As the name implies, it breaks loose from its roots and tumbles wildly around the desert, unless captured by tourists.)

The car trunk was already filled to capacity with nonessentials (according to Dad) my sisters and I had insisted on bringing. So Dad scrounged around for some rope to tie them to the back of the camper.

The three tumbleweeds (we each had to have one) were eventually secured and we went on. Somehow, by evening, they managed to slide down and cover the tail light and license plate.

That was just the beginning. At every campground from Nevada to California and back to Pennsylvania, the first thing Dad had to do was untie the tumbleweeds and retie them to the nearest stationary object. (In spite of that they almost escaped from us in windy Kansas!)

Every morning we heard Dad muttering something about "letting these dumb weeds blow away," and "you *girls.*" But we knew he wouldn't let them escape.

Thousands of miles later we arrived at our home in the Quaker State. In the commotion of unpacking we "temporarily" put the tumbleweeds in the garage. Every summer Dad would ask, "Are you girls going to do something with these tumbleweeds?" Each time we would answer, "We will, Dad, we will."

Five years passed, during which time I was married and moved into an apartment in my parents' house. While cleaning out the garage, my husband came across the unused tumbleweeds. I was still unable to part with them so we decided the attic would be a good storage place.

Another five years passed and Dad rediscovered them in a dark corner of the attic. He brought the largest one downstairs and with a gleam in his eyes said, "Since I went to so much work bringing these pesky weeds home, I'm going to hang one up in our screened-in porch." And that's where it is today.

When I look at the tumbleweed now, I see a lifeless, prickly (some would say ugly), weed—a conversation piece which makes people laugh. I also see, in my mind's eye, my father—a highly organized man—who stopped in the middle of the desert on the whim of his daughters.

That is the kind of parent and friend I would like to be—one who listens, has endless patience, a sense of humor, and sometimes not *too* much common sense. One who, like Christ, is willing to be interrupted. Oh yes, and one with a whole lot of love—how else can you explain carting tumbleweeds across a continent?

In 1989 (after Beth's article was first published), when we sold our house, Beth took the tumbleweed to their new home and hung it up in—of all places!—their garage. Karen rescued her tumbleweed from our attic and it now hangs in their screened-in porch. And Helen, living in Goshen, Indiana, has her tumbleweed in their living room. Perhaps one day Beth's will again have a place of honor. Only then will all three tumbleweeds have reached their "final resting place?" after tumbling about forlornly for more than 20 years!

Growing Together
by Beth Hostetler Mark

Four-year-old Kirstyn announced, "Mommy, when I grow up and get married, I am going to live with you and Daddy."

"Oh no," Mother explained, "when you get married you will move into a house of your own. You won't stay with Mommy and Daddy."

"But Beth is married, and she lives with her Mommy and Daddy!"

Mother and daughter were both right. I am married and I do live with my husband and children in the same house as my parents. However, we have separate living quarters.

For the first seven years of our marriage Ken and I lived in the basement apartment of the house my parents were renting. Two years ago our temporary arrangement became permanent when all four of us bought the house.

Although we co-own the house, my parents made the down payment and are now paying a larger portion of the mortgage. When they retire in ten or fifteen years on a fixed income, and we are more financially able, we plan to reverse our roles. At that time Ken and I will pay the larger share of the mortgage.

Any astute business person will recognize that Dad and Mom could have bought the house themselves and continued renting to us. But with parental love and concern for our financial future, they have generously allowed us to invest in the house with them. Without this arrangement, Ken and I would have been unable to purchase a house for many years.

Within a year of the purchase date we remodelled our living area extensively, changing it into a three-bedroom home, with some of our rooms and the entrance at grade level. Actually, our front lawn is the larger of the two.

Over the years a system of communal living has evolved which respects individual family privacy. We share many things, including the main meal of the day. Cooking is done on alternate days, and the meal is eaten in the cook's kitchen. Mother and I enjoy this break from cooking and meal-planning. Dad enjoys my experimenting with new recipes; Ken savors Mom's pastry. We each have our own kitchen but have the benefit of convenient borrowing of a needed ingredient or utensil.

Picking and processing strawberries has been an annual joint project. Early on a June evening we head out to a nearby strawberry patch and pick (up to 100 pounds when the picking is so good we can't stop!). At home we set up an assembly line process consisting of hulling, washing, sugaring, and freezing the berries. The evening is ended with fresh strawberries and ice cream for a tired but satisfied crew.

Another shared project is canning. From my mother I have learned how to can old family recipes such as bread and butter pickles and pickled beets. A tomato juice recipe which I found has become a new favorite to be passed on to my children.

Entertaining is often done together, and thus people of various ages have come to enrich our lives. At the same time the work of preparation and cleaning up is lessened. We also entertain on our own. When Ken and I have our Bible Study Group at our home, my parents babysit our children, ages two and four.

Some things we share or jointly own save us money. A screened-in porch is the setting for many summer meals cooked on the barbecue grill. We own one vacuum cleaner, a washer and dryer, a lawn mower, and a storage shed with various garden items.

At one time, in addition to our individual cars, we shared a 17-year-old Volkswagen. Later we co-owned a moped which was used for short trips. And after that a succession of other cars. Repair bills have been halved and needless duplication avoided.

Living with different generations has enhanced all our lives. A recent review of the book, *Grandparents/Grandchildren*, speculates that "the time when grandparents served as feeders, caretakers, mentors, and role models seems to be ending." My children have a very close relationship with their grandparents. When Grandma makes pies she often stands at her kitchen counter with Ryan standing on a chair on one side and Sally on the other. Samples of dough are freely given and quickly disappear.

When Ryan began to walk he learned to follow Grandpa around in his workshop. Under his supervision, Ryan hammered hundreds of nails into a scrap of styrofoam. During our remodelling project Ryan was constantly underfoot with his own nail apron and workbench.

Grandpa was never too busy to accept Ryan's "help." Sally has since become an eager volunteer, giving assistance that only a grandparent could appreciate.

My parents enjoy seeing their grandchildren grow and develop from day to day. The authors of the book mentioned above observe correctly that "grandparents and children do not have to do anything to make each other happy. Their happiness comes from being together."

While we remodelled, Ken became an apprentice carpenter, receiving on-the-job training from Dad. Ken, in turn, tinkers with, and has taught Dad, the inner workings of radios, stereos, computers, and other electronic equipment.

Major purchases by either family, such as cars and appliances are discussed by all. Not because we *have* to, but because we value each other's opinions. We also often shop together, which saves gas and encourages us to plan our trips to the store more carefully.

Although Ken and I enjoy being together, we do not share all the same interests. Dad and Ken like watching sports on television or working on a building project together. Mother and I occasionally go to a play or concert. Dad and I share an interest in writing, and we appreciate the convenience of having a willing critic nearby.

The companionship of my parents has made it possible for my children and me to more easily endure Ken's part-time job which keeps him away from home two or three nights a week. On these evenings I am especially grateful for our communal meal time.

After supper Grandpa and Grandma often spend time playing with Ryan and Sally or doing something special such as digging for worms to go fishing. This time gives me a much-needed break from the constant chatter and demands of young children. Conversely, the change of pace helps my parents relax after spending the day working in an office.

My hope for the future is that this complementary sharing will continue. My parents now give an abundance of time and attention to my children. When Ryan and Sally are older, I foresee them helping their grandparents with strenuous chores such as lawn mowing and gardening.

On a different level, the wisdom that comes with age and the enthusiasm of youth will provide good learning experiences for all of us.

As a pastor my father always counseled newlyweds against living with their parents. He had observed that such attempts almost always ended in hurt feelings and estrangement. He credits our success to Ken's ability and willingness to adjust to the idiosyncracies of three "Hostetlers" rather than one.

We are three generations living together under one roof, yet separately. In an age of conflict, our togetherness is a priceless commodity. I treasure it.

Beth wrote the above article more than ten years ago. Lela and I concur heartily with everything she said. In the fall of 1989 Messiah College purchased our campus home to fit in with their long range expansion plans. And thus our happy family arrangement of living together in one double house came to an end.

We moved into a cottage at Messiah Village, a retirement community owned by our denomination. It gives us the freedom of coming and going at will.

Ken and Beth, of course, needed to find another home. Since Ken has taught school in the Mechanicsburg system (where their children have also attended), and since Beth is a librarian at Messiah College, they decided to find a dwelling in the same school district.

The stipulation Ryan and Sally made was "Let's be sure to get a house near Grandpa and Grandma's place." And so, they became the third generation to place a firm stamp of approval on the communal living plan Beth wrote about.

After looking at many houses, Beth and Ken finally found the one they liked best on a quiet street near a park—with its back lawn nestled up against a Messiah Village lawn! They are within easy walking distance of our home. With the willing permission of the cottage owners involved, we walk through their lawns to each other's homes frequently.

Even Mindy, Ken and Beth's Boston Terrier, has learned the way. One day she disappeared from their lot while they were busy doing lawn work. After looking all around, they decided she must have come to our place. Sure enough, there Mindy was, sitting on our front porch, waiting to be admitted. Unfortunately, we were not at home.

As this was being written, it was springtime. Ken, Beth, Ryan, and Sally walked over to our cottage one night and planted all our flowers while we were away and cared for them until we returned home. To the grandchildren, it just seemed like the natural thing to do.

When we returned to Pennsylvania in early July, a building project awaited us. Beth and Ken were having a foundation installed for a 16 by 24 addition to their house—a winterized screened-in porch/dining room. Within 24 hours after we arrived, Lela and I were involved in construction. For us grandparents, it just seemed like the natural thing to do.

This time Ryan, then 14, was the apprentice carpenter. And Sally helped her grandmother and mother in the kitchen. It's interesting, isn't it, how "things that go around, come around." It just seems like the natural thing to do.

My Most Moving Holiday Tradition
by Beth Hostetler Mark

My family always celebrates the true meaning of Christmas on Christmas Eve, when we read the Christmas story.

The day may include several different activities. Sometimes there are last minute gifts to buy. Sometimes we bake Christmas cookies or go sledding. Sometimes we travel all day and arrive at the home of relatives after dark. When we are at home, we always attend the Candle Light Service at our church.

But without fail we end the day by participating in our annual Christmas Eve ritual.

After every Christmas gift has been placed with care under the colorfully lit tree, we quietly assemble around the oldest man present—recently my father, in times past my grandfather.

With Bible close at hand Dad, now also a grandparent, or my grandfather, leads us in a few well-known carols. The children (at one time my cousins, sisters, and I—now my children, nephews, and niece) magically calm down in anticipation of the traditional reading of shepherds coming to the babe in the manger.

When the carols have ended, we listen to the story from the King James Version of the Bible. A few years after Dad became a grandfather, he began using our children's book which had the ancient story accompanied by many pictures. This has held the children's interest more effectively.

Each year a picture has been taken of the grandchildren clustered around Dad, with someone holding a piece of paper indicating the year. The reading finished, we remain solemn as family members reflect aloud on the meaning of Christmas, Christmases of years past, and our precious family ties.

Our ritual is concluded with prayer, after which the gifts are opened. As a child I always felt impatient, like my four-year-old nephew Vaughn who, when asked if he could be quiet for a moment longer as we all prayed together, said, "Oh Grandpa, just pray 'God is great'" (a four-line prayer!) We all laughed, but even then, I sensed the feeling of continuity and peace that happens every year.

My four-year-old son Ryan has already "caught" the spirit. As we decorated our tree this year, he found that storybook and asked Grandpa to read it.

When we participate in this tradition, the mind of each recalls earlier Christmas Eves, all different, yet all the same.

I think back to a poignant Christmas Eve when we wanted to hold on to every moment because my young cousin Lynn had leukemia. The story of God sending his child to earth had special significance and hope for us that year. When the next Christmas Eve was celebrated, Lynn had flown away to be with the child and Lord of Christmas.

In the recent past we celebrated with joy and wonder as four years in succession we had a new infant cousin join the family circle. The "babe lying in a manger" began to touch us in a very personal way.

Last year we had tears in our eyes during the Christmas story, knowing that my sister and her family would be in Japan as missionaries for the next four years. We didn't want the togetherness to end.

This Christmas our family will be in three different countries—Japan, Canada, and the United States. My parents and my immediate family will be in Canada. I will be experiencing a nostalgic journey to the past as we go to the farm of my grandparents, now in their late 80s, for the first Christmas Eve there in 15 years. Once again I will hear Grandpa Swalm read from the second chapter of St. Luke as he did in my earliest childhood memories.

My sister Helen will be with her husband's family in Pennsylvania. Along with their celebration will be sadness due to the recent death of a grandmother.

My other sister Karen and family in Japan will enjoy Christmas in an unfamiliar culture. It will be exciting, yet tinged with homesickness.

Though far apart on Christmas Eve, the threads of our

tradition will lovingly bind us together. Our thoughts will turn towards Bethlehem and each other as we once again are moved by the words, "And it came to pass in those days...."

Chapter 9

Had Falcon... Did Travel

In 1960 six people decided to take a trip to the West Coast from Western New York. They wanted to see as much of the U.S. as possible while spending the least amount of money.

My wife Lela and I supplied the transportation, driving our new Falcon (compact size) station wagon and charging the others $50 each. All side trips were to be paid for in addition at the rate of one cent per person per mile. Even in those days that was a real bargain.

The only problem—our vehicle was a bit on the small side, as was the 90-horsepower engine. It had a bench seat in front, and another folding bench seat with narrow seat and narrow backrest in the back.

We were six full-size adults:

Orvin White was a lanky minister from Virginia, then pastoring in Massillon, Ohio. Sharon Weisser was a single

75

girl from Clarence Center, New York, with lots of energy. (She wrote up a blow-by-blow account of the trip, and I am using her well written narrative as the basis for this chapter. When quotation marks are inserted, her words are being used.)

Nancy Haun was also a single girl, slender and tall, and also from Clarence Center. JR was my brother, Eli Hostetler, Jr., who was pastoring a church in Ashland, Ohio. Our family decided to call him JR more than 50 years ago, long before the JR Ewing of Dallas fame. Lela Hostetler (my wife) was the mother-figure of the group. As for me, I was pastoring in Clarence Center.

All of us were slightly above average in size, intelligence, sense of humor, conversational gifts, and ability to get along with others. There were, however, all too frequent digressions downward from these qualities.

"Our goals? Well, to see all of the United States (almost all), get plenty of rest—eight hours every night, have relaxed and leisurely meals, . . . and learn to know one another better. Our time allotment was two weeks, one day, two hours, and 48 minutes."

And so the four of us who were from Clarence Center began our trip on Friday, June 3, 1960, heading toward Ashland, Ohio, where we would rendezvous with Orvin and JR. We arrived without incident, and stayed in JR's home for the night.

The next day dawned bright and clear. We all got into our small wagon, but WAIT, someone was missing. Orvin had been scheduled to roll in at 6 a.m. He finally arrived. Apparently he had trouble combing his hair into place. "Our Falcon was packed (and I mean packed!), and we were off as the strains of 'California, Here I Come' were attempted by a few brave souls."

We spent the afternoon telling jokes and driving the streets of Indianapolis. We went through it from southeast to southwest first, then made a wrong turn and went through it from southwest to northeast, and finally went through a third time from northeast to northwest. It was a very hot day, there was no bypass, and we had no air conditioning in the car.

"Toward evening we came into Springfield, Illinois. Here was to be our first sightseeing—the home of Abraham Lincoln. But it was closed. We took some pictures and peered through the windows."

On Sunday we had a worship service as we travelled, with JR leading our discussion. When we stopped at a service station, Nancy and Orvin were arguing as to who was the fastest runner.

"They were each ready to prove their ability. Ready! Set! Go! And they were off! All of a sudden Nancy, who was wearing a straight skirt, began to stumble. Down she went with a laugh and a rip! She got up, a little more slowly than she went down. We were all a bit embarrassed because Nancy fell for a married man."

Late that morning we crossed the wide Mississippi River and visited the Mark Twain home in Hannibal, Missouri. Wonder of wonders, it was open!

We stopped for lunch at a scenic park. It was a bit cool, and Orvin, "showing his true Virginia blood, was cold." Nancy lent him her coat, and it fit very well except that his elbows were showing.

That afternoon we started a war that lasted the rest of the trip—the game Battleship. Just imagine five people, cramped in a small car, holding their Battleship pages so that no one else could see them. But there was an even bigger problem—Orvin's drawling accent. He would say something like "Put a nan in A fave" (all "a" sounds as in hat), meaning, "Put a nine in I-five."

"Toward evening we arrived, war-torn, at Abilene Kansas. We walked up to Ike's [President Eisenhower] home of birth and found it had closed—a few minutes before. The museum was closed too." I backed into the street at the Eisenhower home to take a picture—right into the path of a coming car. "But with our luck of missing things, that car was destined to miss Paul!"

Our next stop was the Brethren in Christ Church in

Abilene, where Ike attended as a boy. We planned to visit the pastor and his wife, but we missed them. (It was becoming a pattern.) We did get into the church and looked around.

We ate our lunch in an Abilene restaurant. Orvin discovered that he didn't have a motel reservation for that night. Declared Orvin, "I'm so unlucky that if it rained soup, I'd be standing outside with a fork!" But his luck changed for the better temporarily; he found a room.

On Monday we arrived in Denver, Colorado, around noon. JR said that he knew of a little place not far west of Denver where he had eaten ten years before. "It's just beyond this curve.... Well, I think it's over this hill....It's not too far from this downgrade," said JR. This went on for miles as our stomachs growled ever more loudly. Finally we saw it—"Ye Olde Joint."

It was well worth waiting for—a cozy little place set among the towering Rockies. When we got out of the car, some of us felt dizzy. "The scientists of the group (the men) came to the conclusion that it was the altitude." The women blamed our lack of food.

Soon after our meal, we went through Berthode Pass, with an altitude of 13,000 feet. It was the high point of our trip. Well, at least it was the maximum altitude.

After supper at Steamboat Pass, we travelled on. At dusk a large deer suddenly jumped on the highway from the right side, and stopped—in our lane! I had a split second to make a decision and decided to veer to the right, behind the deer.

Then it stepped back and turned its head. Both deer and car seemed doomed. But at the last possible moment it saw our car and leaped forward for its very life. Our group felt like "wing and a prayer" survivors..

I was so shaken I stopped at a service station about a half mile down the road. The man there told us a lot of deer-battered vehicles had stopped there through the years. We fervently thanked our Lord for his protection.

About this time Orvin began complaining about saddle sores. They persisted for the rest of the trip, and he seemed to derive a lot of pleasure talking about them.

"As we kept going further west, it was necessary to set our watches back. This (according to the women) made the days longer and the nights shorter. But, they claimed, on the way back the days would be shorter and the nights longer. There's some logic there, but it eluded the male minds."

The fellows all bought ten gallon hats and tried to walk bow-legged. Now, they thought, they would never be spotted as tourists. But Orvin's accent was their Achilles heel. Authentic cowboys just don't come from Virginia.

We highly enjoyed the beauty of the buildings and grounds in Temple Square in Salt Lake City. And, wonder of wonders, we were in time for the organ recital. Our Mormon tour guide was so personable we were almost converted, but JR's skepticism saved us.

In the motel that night Sharon found a whiskey bottle with some whiskey still in it. Later the bottle showed up in Orvin's suitcase!

The next forenoon we reached Las Vegas, where we saw hordes of people fighting with the one-armed bandits. "It was a pitiful sight. The people were enslaved by these machines." We kept an eye on Orvin and JR. The rest of the trip Orvin bemoaned the fact that he had not won a fortune in the sinful city.

By the time we arrived at Hoover Dam, the temperature was scorching. We met some very conservative fellow believers. Lela was fearful that they would be offended with her recently purchased, rather garish hat which proclaimed "Life is just a bowl of cherries!" Sharon struggled to keep her skirt down in the gusts of wind.

That afternoon JR asked Nancy to promise she would keep a rattlesnake if he caught one. She promised, with her hand on a stack of wrinkled clothes. "Well, when we stopped at the next gas station, JR came back with a snake in his hands. Sharon screamed, but Nancy resolutely went to JR and held out her hands. The snake was made of rubber."

After driving through the desert, we arrived in

Upland, California, our destination. We all scattered to friends and relatives except Sharon. Arrangements had been made for her to stay in the home of the mother of the Mayor of Upland. She was a very proper Christian lady indeed. After arriving there, Sharon was shown to her room. With her hostess standing by, she threw her suitcase on the bed and flung open the lid. There, in plain view lay the condemning evidence of the partly empty whiskey bottle!

For the next number of days the group attended our denominational conference. Some yielded to temptation and visited, among other places, Knotts Berry Farm, Disneyland, the baseball park, Long Beach, etc.

"The final session of the conference was late in the afternoon. We were ready to hit the road, but Paul discovered a flat tire on the Falcon. The tire had a screw driver in it." We finally got away about 7:30 and drove through the desert all night—toward the southern rim of the Grand Canyon.

The only excitement of our weary, hot journey was hitting a jack rabbit. Our motley crew reached the canyon rim about daybreak. Paul jumped out and called for the rest to follow. The other two men responded, but the women wouldn't/couldn't move from their seats.

But they came suddenly alive when JR, standing on a rocky ledge, lost his balance. With flailing arms and a loud yell, he disappeared over the edge. The three women felt sick, seeing in their mind's eye a crumpled body thousands of feet below. They prayed "panic prayers."

Just then they saw a cowboy hat and JR's grinning face come slowly into view. The women were not amused.

After visiting the Petrified Forest and admiring the Painted Desert, we drove to Farmington, New Mexico. The motel there was the best of our trip, and it had a pool. Orvin, as usual, had bad luck—no trunks. He considered plunging in "as is," but thought better of it. Sharon lent him the bottoms of her mother's two-piece bathing suit. It had been made for wide hips; Orvin's were narrow. When Orvin went off the diving board, we all closed our eyes.

Our next stop of note was Dodge City, Kansas. JR and Orvin settled all their problems there by shooting it out at Boot Hill. We were emotionally prepared to bury one or both of them with their boots on. But they were such poor gunmen that they missed all six shots (with cardboard guns). Thereupon they shook hands and climbed back into the wagon.

"We had far to go and time was escaping. The now long awaited hours which were to be added to the night were not added but just taken off the night. The days weren't longer like they were on the way out, but the nights were just shorter." If you can understand Sharon's reasoning, you are really bright!

The rest of the trip went by in a kind of blur. In our travels we had solved most of the world's problems, including the building of a bridge across the Atlantic Ocean. The Pacific, we had decided, was too wide.

As we drove our last few miles we viewed the very ordinary landscape near our homes. One of Sharon's final comments was "Be it ever so humid, there's no place like home!"

Chapter 10

In the First Place

In most of this book narratives are shared without regard to chronology. Advisors have suggested, however, that some attention be given to relating events in the order they happened. So the next three chapters are an attempt to comply with their request.

Lela and I were each born into a preacher's family in the mid-twenties. Lela first saw the light of day in a farm home near Duntroon, Ontario, Canada. Since Duntroon, as one visitor put it, "has both city limit signs on the same post," let me add that it is near Collingwood and the famous Wasaga Beach on the southern end of Lake Huron.

Her father, the late Dr. E. J. Swalm, in time became a bishop in the Brethren in Christ Church. His great-grandfather came to Canada from Germany and homesteaded on five acres of Crown land. After enduring extended hardship he eventually was able to buy 100 acres of land, and succeeding generations lived there (about five miles south of Collingwood, a city on the Georgian Bay of the lake).

Lela was not in good health when young, being sick about half the time until she was eight. Baptized in a small creek at age 11, she joined the church the same day. She attended the Duntroon elementary school, walking two miles each way. (Perhaps the long walks were what eventually restored her health!) She was a good student and a skillful ball player.

She always looked forward to attending the traditional Love Feasts of her congregation. These two-day events combined preaching, personal testimonies of conversion experiences, feet-washing, communion, and lots of good food at the meals. Lela's favorite food was rivel soup, a delicious dish made in big kettles. Only she can tell you what the "rivels" were.

The Love Feasts were big social occasions, with many people coming from other congregations. It was an excellent opportunity to make new friends.

Some "outside" people did not understand what "Love Feast" meant. One day Charlie Wright, a young man from another church near Stevensville, was taking a carload of friends to a Love Feast across the border in Clarence Center, New York. When they arrived at the Peace Bridge, the customs officer asked where they were going.

"To the Clarence Center Church," said Charlie.

"And what is the purpose of your visit?"

"We're going to a Love Feast."

The officer paused, carefully looking over the group of clean cut young men in the car. Then he smiled and waved them on. "Have a good time, boys, have a good time!"

When Lela came to her high school years, she attended Ontario Bible School (today Niagara Christian College), a church high school beside the Niagara River near Fort Erie, Ontario. The town is across the river from Buffalo, New

York. Among other extra-curricular activities, she was a member of the OBS Ladies Quartet.

That quartet recently got together at their 50th class reunion and sang at the Alumni Dinner. They looked a bit more "mature," but they could still sing very well.

In 1939 Canada became involved in World War II. After her graduation in the spring of 1940, Lela's father asked her to stay at home to help on the farm. Six years went by. During those years she often was the chauffeur for her father as he went to area churches. She also took him to the train station when he went farther afield to preach for revival meetings or to serve in general denominational administration

(As for my childhood days, that information is covered in my most recent book, *Preacher on Wheels*. Here is a brief summary: I was born near Hartville, Ohio, in 1925, the second of nine children. My older sister died when I was three. As a result, I have always felt like the oldest child.)

Lela enrolled at Messiah College, in Grantham, Pennsylvania, in the fall of 1946. Because of delays in getting the proper papers to live across the border, she arrived late. The first two weeks she was lonely and homesick, and would have gone home if there had been any acceptable way.

I was a senior in high school at Messiah that year (Messiah was both a high school and liberal arts junior college.) I was immediately attracted to her, partly because my father was a great admirer of her father, Bishop Swalm. But I soon learned that she had a boyfriend back in Ontario.

When the Gospel Team officers were elected for the next school year, Lela was elected treasurer and I was chosen as president. The following summer (1947) she and her boyfriend decided to call it quits.

That fall she and I began working together. When we had our first meeting, we talked about our new responsibilities in a very matter of fact way, but the atmosphere was charged with electricity. Not long after, Lela and I had our first date.

One evening, during the winter revival meetings at Messiah, we went to Harrisburg after the meeting to pick up Emma Climenhaga, one of the college faculty. When we arrived, her hosts were serving tea and pastries, and we were invited to join them. Mrs. Climenhaga and her friends talked at length, and it began to get late. As a result, we arrived back at the campus after 10 p.m., the zero hour for all girls to be back in the dorms.

But we were in luck. The revival meeting had lasted beyond that hour because seekers were still praying at the altar and being assisted there. Mrs. Smith, the Dean of Women, who exacted fines when girls were brought in late, was still in the chapel.

Not long after that night, I again brought Lela back after the deadline. This time Mrs. Smith was ready for me. After she sent Lela to her room, she scolded me and asked for 25 cents, the amount of the fine. All I had was a 50-cent piece. She didn't have the change, so I told her to keep it for the next time. To my dismay, my remark did not tickle Mrs. Smith's funny bone.

Another time Lela and I sat together at a missionary farewell service in Harrisburg without the proper permission. Unfortunately, Mrs. Smith was there, with her eagle eye. She grounded both of us for a number of weeks. This was a serious problem because Lela and I had a trip scheduled to Washington, D.C. I begged Mrs. Smith to relent, but without success.

Dad always said that when you want action, go to the top. So I made an appointment with the college president. (Ah, to be young and presumptuous again!) The president listened carefully to my tale of woe, and then "ungrounded" us. It may have been because the main purpose of our trip to Washington was to say farewell to two of our missionary friends at the train station. As you can easily detect, our dates were "daring flings."

In spite of the various roadblocks placed before us, Lela and I continued our courtship, and in the spring of 1948, right after her graduation from Junior College, I asked her to marry me. She hesitated for what seemed like long moments (the proper thing in those days) and then said she had been thinking and praying about the matter, just in case I ever asked her. Her answer was a firm Yes. Joy of joys!

She went home to Canada and our courtship by letters began. All that summer and all my following year at Messiah as a college sophomore, she wrote faithfully, six days a week, so that I would receive a letter each day the mail was delivered.

I'm forced to admit that I didn't do nearly as well; most weeks I wrote three letters, with my typewriter (so she would be able to read them). One day I double spaced my letter, cut each line out separately, and pasted the ends together. It was the "longest" letter I ever wrote.

When Lela was handed that letter, she was on the tractor, ready to pull a wagon to the field. She opened the envelope as she was driving, and to her embarrassment parts of my long letter tumbled in various directions. If she hadn't stopped, some of my passionate lines would have been destroyed forever under the wheels of a Ford tractor!

Shortly before my graduation from Junior College (all that Messiah offered at that time) in the spring of 1949, I was asked to become the associate pastor at the Clarence Center, New York, church. John Hostetter (no relation) was the pastor. I accepted and moved into the parsonage with John and his wife Nellie soon after Commencement.

Lela and I were married on August 17, 1949, in the Sixth Line Church, near Stayner, Ontario. The summer had been very hot, and the lawns were brown everywhere because of extended dry weather. The spring, which had for many years supplied plenty of water for the Swalms and their livestock, went dry. The women thought this was a terrible crisis because the reception was going to be held at the Swalm home. But sufficient water was hauled in. I was too dazed to give it much thought.

The wedding rehearsal was scheduled for the night before the wedding. My best man and others were coming from Pennsylvania. About the time they were expected to arrive, we received a phone call from Fort Erie, four hours away. They had been delayed! And so we waited for them, concluding the rehearsal after midnight. We did set one record, I suppose of questionable merit: both our rehearsal and wedding were on the same day.

The wedding ceremony, performed by both our fathers, went smoothly. After the final prayer, we walked down the aisle with joy and relief. When we reached the vestibule, however, an usher leaned over to me and said that we might as well cooperate with the next "plans."

To our amazement, a small truck was backed up right to the church door, and it had a cutter on it (a small, one-horse sleigh). We were informed that we should get on it, or else we would be placed there. My first feeling was outrage, and Lela's was dismay. But seeing no way of escape, we climbed onto the seat and were soon on our way "in great triumph" (for the instigators of the ride).

My best man jumped into a car and followed the truck. When we came to the first stop sign, Lela and I jumped off the cutter and ran to the car. And so began our first hour of wedded bliss.

After living in the John Hostetter home for the first four months of our married life (where we learned that the only way to eat apple pie is with lots of milk), we moved into an upstairs apartment on Railroad Street in Clarence Center. An older woman lived on the first floor. The rumor was that she was very hard to get along with, but we learned to love her dearly.

Mr. and Mrs. Baez lived next door. He was a noted physicist at Bell Aeronautics in Buffalo. The word going around was that he was an FBI agent. Their little daughters were Pauline, Joan, and Mimi. As many readers know, Joan later became world-famous as a folk singer. They were wonderful neighbors.

While we lived on Railroad Street, our first child Beth was born in 1950, and Karen was born in 1951. For some reason, when Lela came home from the hospital with Karen,

I needed to carry her (Lela) up the long flight of stairs (no landing). This effort almost destroyed me; I probably haven't fully recovered to this day!

Lela broke a rib just before Karen was born. She was kneeling beside our bed for prayer one night, and when she got up a rib snapped. We have both wondered if anyone else ever cracked a rib as a result of kneeling to pray.

In those three years I worked as a carpenter, starting at $1.40 an hour and working up to $1.75 by the summer of 1952. I also drove an oil truck one winter.

We were very "hard up." Lela did her best to stay under $5.00 a week for groceries, and usually succeeded. The first Christmas we bought gifts for each other at the Bratt General Store on the "square" of Clarence Center, and charged them. I bought Lela a Sunbeam toaster, and she bought me a Remington electric shaver. Our surprises for each other taxed our finances severely.

We arranged to pay for the love gifts at the rate of a dollar or two a week. It took a long time. Lela was often amused by the quaint, aged Mr. Bratt. But that toaster, purchased more than 40 years ago, is still working fine! Our children, as they got older, loved to go to Mr. Bratt's store, press their noses up against the glass cases, and select one or more pieces of candy for a single cent.

In those years I also tried to pay back the money the Home Mission Board had loaned me for my college tuition. One day I asked the board what my balance was. The treasurer informed me that there was no balance due; someone had paid the whole thing. In the years which followed, I suspected first one person, and then another, and another. It is a wonderful feeling to be sweetly suspicious of anonymous benefactors.

Chapter 11

All I Know About Women

During the first three years we served the Clarence Center Church, Messiah College had become a four-year, degree-granting college. Following what we believed to be the Holy Spirit's direction, we moved into a new apartment on the campus of Messiah College the fall of 1952 and I enrolled as a junior.

Beth was two and Karen one. The apartment had one room only. To conserve space I made bunk cribs. One day the college president brought the Board of Trustees to have a look at our apartment. The children were asleep in the cribs *before* they knocked on the door. The President informed the trustees that we had *three* children. Lela saw them peering around carefully for the third one! The only other spaces were the closet and bathroom!

To help with expenses, Lela did laundry for the college fellows, and I got carpenter jobs. I also pastored the small Rana Villa Church nearby where I received a monthly offering. This small offering was always larger when we put a generous amount in it!

Toward the end of the two years, Lela became pregnant with our final daughter Helen. It was my privilege to graduate with honors and be selected as one of the student commencement speakers.

I failed, however, to get the highest honors in the class and felt like the graduate whose classmates were graduated Summa Cum Laude, well ahead of him. He looked up to heaven and cried, "Oh Laude, how cum!"

Some months before the commencement exercises of 1954, the Clarence Center Congregation invited us to return as their pastoral couple. We were given $250 a month and the use of the parsonage. The residence for pastoral families was spacious but we had very little furniture to fill it. When Bishop Henry Miller came to visit us the first time, we offered him the one chair we had in the large living room.

Helen was born that fall. On our way home from the hospital, we were involved in a small accident (in the days before infant seats were required). When I slammed on the brakes, baby Helen fell to the floor. We picked her up quickly and were relieved to see that she was still fast asleep.

Our Christmas card that year had three little angels on it named Beth, Karen, and Helen. Once in a while they even lived up to their billing!

The parsonage kitchen was very "un-modern," with an open sink, narrow counters, and glass panes in the doors. In spite of those limitations, our children liked that kitchen best because "Mother was always there to welcome us home from school."

At Christmas time I asked the older girls to assist me in picking out a dress for their mother. Our choice was a failure; Lela never wore it. It reminded me of a book her father, Bishop Swalm, showed me soon after we were married. It was titled *All I Know about Women*. When I opened the book, all the pages were blank.

The second year at the Clarence Center church Lela and I realized that we could not "make ends meet" with our income. I therefore asked the church board for permission to drive a school bus each morning. With that arrangement I could be in the church office by 9:00 a.m.

This seemed to work out well, but the board and congregation were displeased. They had been proud to have their first "full-time pastor," and now that had been changed. The board soon took action to offer me a raise equal to what I was receiving for driving the bus. I accepted and that was the last time I ever needed to moonlight.

That winter, however, we found that our heating bills for the oil furnace at the parsonage were difficult to pay. The house had natural gas piped into it and a space heater was in the basement. We moved the heater to the living room, hooked it up without a vent, and had it burning 24 hours a day. Gas was cheap, and we were saving a lot of money.

Our deacon, Joe Miller, was deeply concerned that something might cause the flame to fail, resulting in either an explosion or our suffocation. As a result of his urging, the church offered to pay the fuel bill on the condition that we would no longer use the space heater. We accepted, gratefully. Later the church paid for all the utilities. They were good, caring people, and our longest pastoral stay was with the Clarence Center Congregation.

Beth was our first one to march off to school. She entered kindergarten in 1955 and was a good student from the first. Karen enrolled the following year. It soon became evident that she had artistic leanings (she did the line art for this book).

We scraped together enough dollars and bought Beth a 16-inch bicycle early in her school years. One day she came home in a big hurry—probably to rush to the bathroom—and flung down her bike in the driveway, right behind our car. I came out of the house, walked across the front of the car, and backed over the shining bike.

It was a terrible experience for the little lass, and she wept in anguish. Then I told her that if she helped me, we would restore the mangled frame and wheels. We worked on it for a long time. The hardest part was to get the wheels straightened out. We finally coaxed them to the point that, even though they wobbled, they did not rub against the sides of the forks.

One day she went to the nearby store in Clarence Center for an ice cream cone, riding her bike. When she started to pedal home, a pothole in the street caused the ice cream to pop out of the cone. Beth stopped and picked up the dirty ice cream, remounted her bike, and came home in tears.

By the time she reached our house, the ice cream was dripping and the skin of her palm was frozen (it later peeled off). She was comforted by her mother, given another nickel (the first one was Beth's), and sent back to the store. This time she walked.

The year 1961 was the most difficult of our 25 years in pastoral ministries. Being young and inexperienced, I made too many administrative blunders. The congregation asked me to resign and they began looking for another pastor.

Their decision hit us like a bombshell. It seemed like our world was falling apart. We were forced to leave the community where all three of our daughters had been born. Our hearts were heavy, and the road ahead looked bleak indeed. (All this happened more than 30 years ago, and this is the first time I have been able to face it in print.)

Much as we wanted to undo what had happened, the Clarence Center years, with all their hundreds of good memories, were firmly in the past. That July we loaded our belongings on a rental truck and crossed the border into Canada—"on a wing and a prayer."

We were called to serve a small congregation of 15 members in Toronto. Our plan was to move our earthly possessions in a large, rented Hertz van which we reserved well in advance in Niagara Falls, Ontario.

The day we went to pick it up, we learned that the

company had rented the van to someone else. All that was left for us was a truck with wooden side racks and a canvas over the top. That created a serious problem in customs clearances because the truck could not be officially sealed.

One consequence was that we were late in returning the truck. They said we would need to pay a penalty. Then Milly, Lela's younger sister, came to our rescue—with a vengeance! She marched into that Hertz office, asked for the manager, and told him in no uncertain terms that we would NOT pay the penalty because of their giving us the wrong truck. A very subdued manager said, "Let's just forget about the whole thing."

When the truck was fully loaded at Clarence Center, the three bikes belonging to our girls were still on the ground. We got some rope and tied them to the sides of the truck.

They might just as well have been left behind. The first day the girls rode them in Canada, their friends saw the balloon tires and said derisively, "Does your dad work in a balloon factory?" All Canadian bikes had "skinny" tires.

The three bikes were pushed into our garage to stay. We later gave them all away and then purchased used ones with the proper tires at a bike shop. Peer pressure is much more effective than parent pressure, we learned.

Our first home in Toronto was near our church on Gamble Avenue, no less! Helen was seven. Before our furniture was unloaded, she had found a new friend right across the street. She asked Helen about her religious status.

Helen came rushing into our house. "Are we *capital* or *promisen*?" she breathlessly asked her mother.

Lela was amused. "Tell your friend that you are a *Protestant*."

A year later we moved to Budea Crescent, a suburban location, in anticipation of building a new church in a nearby housing development. The girls all attended a new school, Terraview Heights, and did well. Lela and I became actively involved in the PTA organization, a move that, surprisingly, made our girls proud.

A Christian builder in the nearby Bridlewood Development reserved a lot for a church building. His policy was to give such lots to evangelical congregations who, without that kind of assistance, would not be able to build. We qualified and received the lot.

The property on Gamble Avenue was sold, after a handful of legal hassles, and construction began at 480 Huntingwood Drive. That account takes up another chapter of this book.

During the Bridlewood Church years I wrote my first book, published by Baker Book House in Grand Rapids, Michigan. It was written for teens and was titled *You're in the Teenage Generation*. The title, as many will recognize, was a take-off on the commercial, then new, "You're in the Pepsi Generation."

My royalty was five cents a book. Even though the book sold 6,000 copies, I never received enough money to pay for my air ticket to Grand Rapids to negotiate with the Baker Book House editors.

After our girls had lived through their teen years, they told me I should write another book for teens—"because now you know what you are talking about!" I never wrote another teen book. This reminds me of the man who wrote an article on "Ten Theories on How to Raise Children." Later he had ten children, and *no* theories!

Those were the pajama-party years at our house. After doing almost everything but cuss because of the late-night laughter and screams, I began to put modeling clay in my ears. It was both comfortable and effective.

One day Karen organized a neighborhood "Chuck, Chuck Club" for Helen and her friends. They banned all boys and made many kinds of crafts, which they then sold. Later, after we moved to Bridlewood, Karen made large crepe paper flowers and sold them to a local crafts store. Is it any wonder that today she and her husband are in a thriving business selling "Country Gifts 'n Such"?

Our daughters helped us in the church as teachers, and Beth played the piano. Although they vowed never to marry a minister (too much work, too poor pay), they have later been involved in church ministries as a missionary, or deacon, or trustee, and in many other ways. As far as I can tell, they might just as well have married a preacher; they couldn't be any more active in church work.

Beth attended Niagara Christian College during some of her high school years, and was a vital part of their successful basketball team. Because the school was a hundred miles from our home, I never saw her play. She was disappointed, and I deeply regret my omission to this day.

Chapter 12

Exchanging a Boat for a Camper

Also during the Bridlewood years one of the members, an industrial arts teacher in the local high school, was the instructor for an adult night class making fiberglass hulls for small sailboats. One of the hulls came out a bit less than perfect, and no one in the class wanted it. So he gave it to me.

I worked long and carefully, in our basement, to put all the needed mahogany trim on the boat. It had a metal mast and a nylon sail. I made oars and purchased a small motor. My boat worked in any of three ways—sail, row, or motor. It even had a steering wheel and forward-mounted controls.

The family was pleased, but not enthusiastic. They were proud of my accomplishment, but they were not participating. After sailing the boat for two summers, I decided to sell it and get a pop-up camper.

Suddenly the four women in my life came to eager attention! The move from boat to camper was one of the best things Lela and I ever did to promote family togetherness. We all agree on this. We went to our church camp in the Burks Falls area many times, and we loved it.

We travelled all the way to California as a family, and it was one of the high points of our life together. Beth wrote about it in "The Tumbleweed Caper," included elsewhere in this book. Helen says, "I realize now what a financial hardship that trip must have been." She is right, but it was more than worth it.

Later each family became a camping family, and until one camping unit wore out, all three girls and their spouses also owned campers. All of us have worked hard at getting together in a camping setting each year, sitting around the campfire and talking about our other camping experiences, some of them many years ago.

Beth completed Grade 13 while we lived in Toronto, with plans to enroll at Messiah College in the fall of 1969. Early that year I received a call to become the associate pastor of the Grantham congregation, whose church building was on the Messiah College campus.

Lela and I decided to accept the call. The congregation rented a large house for us. It was almost in the center of the campus. It turned out that we lived in that house for 20 years, and we loved every day of it.

Both Beth and Karen enrolled at Messiah that fall—Beth as a sophomore and Karen as a freshman. They had some reservations about "their parents going to college with them," but came to enjoy it wholeheartedly. Among other benefits in their dorm life was the privilege of stopping by with full refrigerator and other privileges. They soon realized that they were having "the best of two worlds." After satisfying their desires in dorm living, they moved back home.

Our daughters all worked hard in both the classroom and at their jobs to help with college bills, both during the school year and in the summer time. With financial assistance from church, state, and federal sources, their many hours of work resulted in their graduation free of any debt.

Soon after they enrolled, Beth and Karen attended a Sunday School class for college students. One of the first topics discussed was the "generation gap." (The Sixties were years of college student rebellion.) The group chose to stay on the topic for extended Sundays. About the fourth Sunday Beth objected. "Karen and I don't see any value in continuing to discuss this topic. We really don't know what you kids are talking about—it has never happened to us."

Lela and I were understandably pleased—yes, very proud of our daughters. We cherish Beth's protest.

The move took Helen to a new school in her second year in high school. The transition was difficult. One crisis involved gathering insects for a good, but very demanding teacher. She needed a net, so I made one for her.

One day I demonstrated how to use it in the lawn between our house and the large college science hall. I dashed hither and yon and after much exertion managed to capture a butterfly. Unnoticed by me, classes had just dismissed and a large crowd of students were witnessing my heroic efforts. When I caught the butterfly, they cheered and applauded! Helen's face was red! Mine was too, but for an additional reason.

The college years were good years for our girls and for us. One day Karen came out of the campus center as I was approaching it. She rushed toward me crying and threw her arms around me. What could be her problem, I wondered uneasily. Once again it was "panic prayer" time.

Failure in a test? Rejection by a friend? An unwanted pregnancy? All of these unhappy possibilities flashed through my mind as I held her in my arms.

She finally wiped her eyes and told me. "I just love you *so much!*," she whispered.

I almost perished with relief! I also was the proudest man in the whole college community that day! And every time I remember Karen's words, I feel my surge of joy all over again.

Lela got a job working in the college library the first fall, and she worked there until she retired. Her 21 years in the Acquisitions Department were very fulfilling. Our daughters, one by one, also worked in the library, both during their school years, and in the summer time.

Beth received the most direct benefit; she went on to a Master's degree in Library Science and is presently working on another Master's degree. She is one of the librarians on the 2200-student campus.

When Beth was working on her first graduate degree, her husband Ken and I were also studying at the same level. He is a teacher and his degree was in education, while I pursued studies in the humanities. It happened that all three of us would complete our work the same spring. And so the race for top honors was on!

Beth won. Both Ken and I were pleased with her performance, but our male pride was injured.

I pastored at the Grantham Church for five years. One day I was flying home from Chicago with the college Dean, Dr. Dan Chamberlain. Right "out of the blue" (we were at 35,000 feet!) he asked me to consider serving as the Information Director at Messiah.

Lela and I were in our 25th year in pastoral ministries. We had been talking about a possible career change for me, either at our college or in missions, but we had not talked to anyone about it. After careful consideration and prayer, I accepted the college offer, working happily in that position for ten years.

In 1984 I accepted a call from the Church to serve as the Associate Director of Stewardship. I continued in that fulfilling responsibility until our retirement in July of 1990. For the next two years Lela and I served as volunteers, traveling to the congregations with a message of stewardship and encouragement.

A retirement epilogue

I typed parts of this book while Lela and I traveled around North America. One of the many places we visited was the Church's Timber Bay Children's Home in Saskatchewan, where I conducted a week of seminars for the 25-person staff.

One day I went fishing with Dale Winger and his two sons in the large Montreal Lake nearby. I had the best fishing experience of my life! With four of us in the boat, at one time three had a fish on the line. We caught so many that we were forced to throw the smaller ones back (under 22-inches) in order to stay under our limit—six fish per person. All were Northern Pike.

We caught the Pike in less than an hour. Cleaning them was another matter, taking much longer. We finally sat down to eat in the Winger home about 9 p.m., still in full daylight! Dale's wife Linda served the fish she had fried with her special recipe. I had the luck of catching the largest one—28 inches long or 71 centimeters (that sounds longer!). We went fishing again two days later and again caught our limit.

On the same day we caught our first fish, two men from the Children's Home went bear hunting, and they came home proudly with two large black bears. The men skinned them, with plans to have bearskin rugs grace their living room floors (depending somewhat, I suppose, on how their spouses felt about such interior decorating). The bear meat provided much good eating. As for me, I prefer to respectfully leave all bears in the woods.

Chapter 13

Saying
the Three Magic Words

Over the years I've collected numerous sayings about parenting and grandparenting.

On being a grandfather: "Old age is not uncomfortable if a man has grandchildren to share it with him . . . "—Scott. "Of all the gifts of God, one of the greatest is the privilege of being a grandfather."—Young. "The father who is old at 40 can turn into a grandfather who is young at 70."—Talmage. "The boy who grows up without a grandfather has only half a childhood." Russian Proverb. "If Mother says no, ask Grandmother; if all else fails, ask Grandfather!"—from a plaque.

On being a grandmother: "A good grandmother can cure most of a family's ills."—Chinese Proverb. A mother works hard at bringing up her children just right—so she can become a grandmother and spoil her grandchildren."—Reddick. "Grandmothers can get along with anybody—with the possible exception of grandfathers."—Thompson. "Grandmothers take all the praise . . . while mothers do all the work."—Boland.

"A grandmother is just like a mother except a grandmother has more time for kids."—Written by a first-grade student. "Each grandmother secretly believes that every new grandchild looks exactly like her."—Newman. "Mothers bear children . . . grandmothers enjoy them."—Spanish Proverb.

All grandparents reading this, although they may not agree, will be fully understanding when I say that our grandchildren are not only the most attractive children we know, but also the most intelligent. Lela and I indulge them shamelessly.

On having daughters: "When a father looks upon a daughter he bears the love that he bore her mother echoed down through the years."—Moore. "There is no kind of affection as angelic as the love of a father for a daughter."—Addison. "The most important part of being a good father to a daughter . . . is to love and respect her mother."—French Proverb. "The lucky man has a daughter as his first child."—Spanish Proverb. "A daughter is the companion, the friend, the confidant of her mother . . . and the object of pleasure, something like the love between the angels, of her father."—Steele.

Open Letters to my Daughters
I find it very hard to express my deepest feelings directly to the persons I love most. Although I've been trying to strengthen this weakness, my success has been rather limited.

And so I am writing these letters to you. Hopefully, they will make up a bit for the words I should have spoken and the many more hugs I should have given each of you.

In another sense, I am writing in behalf of most Dads with daughters. Far too many of us find it difficult to vocalize our feelings—to simply say, "I love you!" Be assured, daughters, that we feel much more than we ever get said. Our reluctance is one of the results of boys learning to repress feelings of pain and love early in life. "To keep such feelings hidden is more masculine" is the message we received. As a result, we and those we love are the poorer.

And so the following is an attempt to hug you with my words and kiss you with my phrases. Perhaps these efforts will help me to do better when we are face to face. I hope so.

Dear Beth:

You are my favorite daughter, and here are some reasons:

You are our firstborn, coming to us from the hand of God early in our marriage.

I can still vividly remember the first time I saw you in the Millard Filmore Hospital in Buffalo, New York. The stresses of your recent birth had pressed your head out of shape. You had very little hair. But the very first time you opened your eyes and looked into mine, I was smitten with such feelings of love that tears came into my eyes.

From that moment on I have never ceased to love you with all my heart.

You developed into a beautiful child, and I suppose others were amused, as I am now, when they observed the undisguised pride of a father with his offspring.

It didn't take long for your mother and me to discover that you were not only beautiful, but also very bright. You gladdened our lives with your smiles and laughter. You challenged us to be better persons, so that you would grow up with good examples before you.

As you grew older, you were constantly reaching out for new challenges. I remember that you wanted to ride a two-wheel bike before I thought you were old enough. We started out together, with me holding up your bike. But soon you pedalled on your own—very wobbly at first, and then straight and unafraid. This, it would seem, is a parable of a good relationship between father and daughter.

I remember your first day of school. It was hard to be sure of your feelings, but from our side of things, you ventured into this new phase of your life with head up and eyes shining. And from that day to this, your efforts in school have always made us proud, very proud.

Early in your school days you gave evidence of being a good writer. Your compositions contained terse and colorful prose. You began an article with clarity and moved in a straight line to the conclusion.

I recall that you entered an essay contest, sponsored by the local Lions Club. You were in Grade 8 in the excellent Canadian school system in Toronto, Ontario. Your article was on the benefits of newspapers. You were stretched out on the floor of our living room, penning your thoughts.

The night the awards were announced, we knew that you had won one of the prizes, but we were proud indeed when your essay was given the top spot! Your picture and essay appeared in the paper the next day.

You gave your heart to the Lord in your tender years, and it was my privilege to baptize you and later to receive you into church fellowship. Those were high days in your and my life.

You grew into young womanhood and found a good, godly man for your marriage partner. Together you and Ken gave us two grandchildren, Ryan and Sally. Today Ryan is taller than his grandmother, and Sally is not far behind. We love them and they love us—even though we are old!

You spend your money wisely, many times searching out used clothes at an area rummage sale. When your friends see you, Ken, and the children dressed so attractively, very few realize that often you are wearing the used clothes you have shopped for with painstaking care.

You have reflected our love for ministry in the local church and at the General Conference level. You and Ken are a deacon couple in the Grantham Church, and both of you have important responsibilities in the administration of our biennial General Conference.

Your position as a Messiah College librarian fits well with your long-time love of reading and your organizational ability.

I could say more, much more. But I do want to say one more time that I love you unabashedly. No father could have a better daughter.

Dear Karen:

You are my favorite daughter, and here are some reasons:

You are Daughter Number Two, coming to us from the hand of God fourteen months after your sister Beth. We were able to enjoy you more because by the time you came we were pros at raising infant girls!

I can still remember the first time I saw you in the Millard Filmore Hospital in Buffalo. The birth process treated you kindly, and your head was "in good shape" from the first. You had beautiful dark hair. After I waited quite a while, you opened your eyes and looked at me. I was thrilled, but you promptly frowned and closed your eyes again. But that short look into your eyes filled me with unutterable feelings of fond affection.

From that moment on I have loved you with utter abandon.

You developed into a beautiful child, and your mother and I were more proud of you than we cared to admit. After all, pride was considered sinful by pious fellow-believers.

It didn't take long for your mother and me to discover that you were not only unusually pretty, you were also very intelligent. You were a bit more serious than Beth, but you brightened our home with your smiles and laughter. You were a very determined young child, and we soon saw that we would need to bring you up with a firm hand.

In your early years you were also a rather fearful child in some ways. More than once you were brought back to us from your first ventures in a Sunday School class setting. You were also reluctant to leave home on your first day of school. But you soon went gladly, and with full confidence.

You began to give evidence of your artistic abilities very early in life, and this continued as a kindergartner. One day you drew a picture which your teacher decided to keep for future display purposes. You, however, wanted to bring it home to show to us. When the teacher refused your request to return it, you marched off to the office of the principal, Mrs. Ebersole. Your plea was effective; the teacher was told to give your picture back! A week or two later Mrs. Ebersole told us about it at a PTA meeting. She was greatly amused—and impressed.

And from that day to this, your artistic productions have always made us proud, very proud.

You accepted Jesus as your Savior while still a child, and it was my profound pleasure to baptize you and later receive you into church membership.

You delighted me with your mechanical and carpentry skills. Today you have a table saw and other power tools, and you are good at using them.

One day in Toronto when I rented a Honda 50cc bike to give you girls rides, you told the neighborhood children that they could have rides too—if their parents signed, and if they paid a small amount for each ride. I gave rides for several hours and did not know until later that you had collected enough money to pay for the bike rental!

You are married to a good, godly man. Together, you and Dan gave us two grandsons, Vaughn and Cameron. We love them both very much.

You and Dan served in Japan as missionaries, making our hearts glad even though we missed you terribly. When you came home, you opened a crafts and antique shop, and are doing well in that business. You have also been much involved in your home congregation in Harrisburg.

I could say much more. Let me say, however, one more time that I love you with all my heart. No father could have a better daughter.

Dear Helen:

You are my favorite daughter, and here are some reasons:

You came to us from the hand of God—our third daughter. You are three years younger than Karen. You hold a very special place in our lives because you are our baby.

I shall never forget the first time I saw you. Beyond any doubt, you were the most beautiful baby in the Millard Filmore Hospital in Buffalo. Well, let me insist that you were tops in the whole city, perhaps even the state of New York! Fathers do get carried away, especially with good evidence at hand!

From that moment on I have never ceased to love you unreservedly.

You developed into a beautiful child, and your father and mother were proud to "show you off" at every possible opportunity. Nowadays I get a bit impatient with fathers who act that way.

You trotted off to kindergarten and did well. We soon discovered that you needed to work a bit harder in school than your sisters, but you came through with good grades for two reasons. First, you developed good study habits. Second, you were especially gregarious, always having plenty of friends.

From your first day of school to the present moment your successes have always made us proud, very proud.

You decided to give your heart to our Lord at your mother's knee, while still a child, and it was my fatherly delight to baptize you and receive you into church membership some years later.

It was a great thrill for us. Now our whole family was/is in the Kingdom of God! This had been the first priority of our life together.

When we moved to Pennsylvania at the end of your first year in high school, the transition was very difficult for you. You came home crying for a number of days because you had not yet found a friend. You had always been good at making friends, but it was much harder as a tenth-grader.

But one day you found another lonely girl, and then another, and you had a great time at the new school after all.

You grew into young womanhood and married a good, godly man. Together you and Rick gave us our "baby" grandchild, special because she is the youngest. Our hearts ached with you through five miscarriages. Each one seemed like the loss of a loved one.

You are very special to us because you are the teacher in our family. That you teach pre-school children is not, in my opinion, an inferior position. In fact, I am convinced that pre-school and kindergarten are the most important years in a child's life. When such children are taught by good teachers, they are well on their way to bigger and better things.

Like your parents, you love your church, and both you and Rick are involved in your local Nappanee, Indiana, congregation in many ways. Your willingness to drive rather far in order to worship in a Brethren in Christ Church pleases us greatly.

One of your endearing qualities is being a bit "klutzy," just like your mother. Her mother got her leg stuck fast in a hole in the barn, your mother has had some falls on totally smooth sidewalks, and you have a way of stubbing your toe against the most innocuous objects! It just runs in the family!

I could go on and on. Perhaps I have missed some things that should have been mentioned. If so, forgive your absent-minded father. But one thing I will never forget. I love you more than words can express. No father could have a better daughter.

After her first miscarriage, Helen wrote the following article, which was never published.

Miscarriage.

It was a word in my vocabulary but not in my experience. Actually, I had rarely even thought about it. Perhaps that was because no one close to me had ever suffered a miscarriage.

And so I supposed that this was something that didn't happen very often, and when it did, it always happened to someone in another family, or county, or state. I never suspected that it would happen to me. But it did.

When my husband Rick and I made plans to start our family, about five years after our marriage, it seemed at first that our wishes would not be fulfilled. But we felt that if our having a baby was God's will, it would happen.

As you can therefore easily imagine, we were overjoyed when we found out that I was pregnant. Rick and I made haste to spread the good news. Many people shared our delight—friends, relatives, and neighbors. The first few months went by in a euphoric glow as we began choosing names and started thinking about what it would be like to be parents.

Then it happened. At the end of twelve short weeks I miscarried the baby. My husband and I were totally unprepared. We felt fear, confusion, and sadness in almost overwhelming proportions.

I was scared because I did not know what was happening to me. So many changes occurred all at once. I kept wondering what went wrong.

I was also confused. Many times I cried and pleaded "Why me, Lord?" So many unwanted babies are born every day. I couldn't understand why God would take away a baby who would have been loved so greatly. I was told that many miscarriages are nature's way of taking care of abnormal fetuses. Somehow this didn't help very much. (I've found out since that one out of five pregnancies ends in a spontaneous abortion—the doctor's term for the unhappy experience.)

The feelings of fear and confusion were gradually replaced by a deep sadness and depression. A part of me had been torn away, and I mourned for the baby I never knew. Rick and I prayed that we would be able to accept our great loss as God's will for our lives. Although it took a while, we were finally at peace with God and ourselves.

I've read about women who remained depressed for months and even years after a miscarriage. Even though some hurt lingers, I am thankful that I was able to come out of my depression relatively quickly. How was this possible? The people who shared our joy also shared our sorrow. Those who rejoiced with us when we rejoiced were now weeping with us as we wept. We felt surrounded by God's love as we received flowers, phone calls, notes, and visits from the many who reached out with loving concern.

I pray that you will never need to experience such a shattering sense of loss. But if you do, let me assure you that you are not alone. There are women around you who have gone through this unhappy occurrence and it helps to talk to them. Many people love you and will be very supportive.

But most important of all—God is always with you.

Chapter 14

"...then the letting go..."

I guess I should have felt good about our daughter Karen going to Japan as a missionary. But I didn't. In fact, I felt very depressed.

It always seemed to Lela and me that it would be wonderful if one of our children were a missionary. But the soft glow of the theoretical was destroyed by the harsh glare of the actual. Karen and Dan (Deyhle) were gone, and with them went two grandsons who were an inexpressible delight to us.

I guess it was partly our fault. In our 25 years of pastoral ministries we often had missionaries in our home. They had interesting stories to tell, and our three girls listened with avid attention. When a reporter asked Karen why she had decided to be a missionary, she gave as one reason: "Missionaries used to come to our home so I heard them talk about their exciting work."

The day Dan and Karen first talked to us about going to Japan, I didn't have much to say. I felt guilty about my lack of enthusiasm, but couldn't seem to feel otherwise although I prayed about it. I confess with shame that my secret hope was that something would happen to prevent their leaving us. But they were more obedient Christians than I, and so they went.

A few days before they left, the Harrisburg congregation had a farewell and commissioning service. Pastor Glenn (Woody) Dalton was in charge. He preached a stirring sermon on the need for everyone in the congregation to be a minister, not just the pastor. Following the message he asked Karen and Dan to come forward, and they made pledges to our Lord which many readers have either heard or themselves made.

He then asked Lela and me to stand beside them. Next he asked the church board to come forward. And finally, he invited others to come as well. Many came. At that moment it struck me as never before—Dan and Karen and Vaughn and Cameron were going. Nothing was going to change that.

Shaken to my innermost being, I began to weep. Now, I very seldom cry, especially in public. My wife is sometimes embarrassed when she thinks I should be shedding tears but don't. I have at times wished I could cry so that others could see how deeply I am feeling.

And then Pastor Dalton asked me to lead in the prayer of consecration. It was one of the most difficult prayers I ever prayed. But God is good, and he helped me.

As always happens, the parting day came. We took the family to the airport and sent them on their way. As someone with previous experience put it, "This is a bitter-sweet time." How true.

Our other grandson, then three years old, had been spending extra time playing with his cousin Vaughn. That night at the dinner table Ryan was forlorn, asking again and again to see Vaughn. He finally realized that Vaughn was gone and would be gone for a very long time. "He's not coming back, is he?" Ryan cried. It was, for me, the low point of the whole day.

How does one get over this version of postpartum depression? My father-in-law, Dr. E. J. Swalm, travelled widely during his active years as an evangelist and church administrator. He was asked how he was able to be away from his wife and family for such long periods of time. "Perhaps you get used to it after a while," someone suggested. The veteran minister shook his head. "It's something I have never gotten used to."

We were told that letters help. And they certainly did. I often thanked the Lord for all the letters that came the years they were away, first in Zambia for a few months and then in Japan.

As I have reflected on the whole matter, I now know that through the years I should have been more supportive of the loved ones left behind by missionaries. It could well be that they suffer more in some ways than those who go to the far shores. I therefore resolved to be more understanding and comforting to the sending ones.

When Dan and Karen began their work in Japan, we became much more interested and involved in Japanese missions. This reminded me of the man who lived beside a large river. He knew that other people lived on the other side of the river, but he really wasn't interested. Then one day his daughter got married and moved across the river. Suddenly what happened on the other side of the river was important to him.

What is more, from time to time he would cross the wide expanse of water to visit her. When I mentioned this at the reception in the Harrisburg Church following the commissioning service, someone asked, "Do you and Lela plan to make a trip to Japan to visit Dan and Karen and your grandchildren?"

"Well," we replied, "we'll cross that bridge when we come to it."

In the meantime, my goal in relation to our painful separation was to arrive at the last clause of Emily Dickinson's poem:

> *After great pain, a formal feeling comes—*
> *The Nerves sit ceremonious, like Tombs—*
> *The stiff Heart questions was it He, that bore,*
> *And Yesterday, or Centuries before?*
> *The Feet, mechanical, go round—*
> *Of Ground, or Air, or Ought—*
> *A wooden way*
> *Regardless grown,*
> *A Quartz contentment, like a stone—*
> *This is the Hour of Lead—*
> *Remembered, if outlived,*
> *As Freezing persons, recollect the Snow—*
> *First—Chill—then Stupor—then the letting go—*

Lela and I did cross the above-mentioned river in the summer of 1983. Bob and Milly Hawes (Lela's sister) travelled with us. They were the very best of travelling companions, and we had a wonderful four weeks together.

We first flew to Los Angeles and spent some days on the West Coast because Bob and Milly had not been there before. Then we flew to Hong Kong, losing a whole day when we crossed the International Date Line. In Hong Kong we tried to resist the pressure, without much success, of eager salesmen who came right out on the street to take us into their stores.

Our main memory of Hong Kong, however, was jet-lag. When we arrived at our hotel I threw myself on the bed and immediately went to sleep. A good while later the phone rang. I got off the bed and staggered over to answer it. It was Milly, calling from their room, and she wondered what we were planning to do next. After a long pause (she says) I replied, very uncertainly, "I'm just looking around."

When I hung up, I looked at myself, still fully dressed, and told my wife in great alarm, "I slept all night with all my clothes on!" She just laughed at my confusion; I had been asleep only a few hours.

After a few days in Hong Kong, we flew to Tokyo, where Dan, Karen, and the boys were waiting for us. We wedged our baggage and ourselves into their mini-van and headed for Karuizawa, a city in the mountains to the north. To our amazement, the Tokyo streets were not named. The reason—to confuse any foreign invaders. Well, we were confused, and Dan had some extended conversations with people he asked. Fortunately, they always very cheerfully gave us directions, with much excitement and arm waving.

We spent some days in a missionary home in Karuizawa, resting, shopping, and visiting Dan and Karen's friends. (Dan and Karen had done their language study there.)

The remainder of our time in Japan was spent in Nagoya, where Dan and Karen were helping to establish a new congregation. We observed and learned many new things. I will now mention some of these.

Japan is very crowded. Mountains cover six of every seven square miles, squeezing the population into the valleys and along the seashores. When we travelled on the fabulous *Shinkosen* ("Bullet Train"), we went through many tunnels because of land scarcity. When I stood at a window to take pictures of the scenes flashing by at 150 miles an hour, I would sometimes press the camera shutter just as we zipped into yet another tunnel.

Such crowded conditions usually breed squalor, ugliness, and crime, but Japan has successfully resisted such tendencies. As we travelled by car and train, the unfolding panorama of valleys, villages, lakes, and mountains was breathtaking.

The rice and tea fields are arranged in picture-book symmetry. The lawns of city homes are very small. Because of limited space, shrubs and trees are grown in miniature. There is often a focal point such as a bamboo fountain, a slanting pine, or simply a rock.

Inside the Japanese homes, the beauty continues. A

flower arrangement usually greets a visitor just inside the door. Perhaps more than any other people on earth, the Japanese love flowers and greenery, and they have given many centuries of careful thought to simple, striking arrangements.

The *gaigin* (outsider) feels very foreign among the Japanese. Visitors stick out like sore thumbs. As we moved about in the crowded streets, stores, and stations, we felt very isolated. Children, and occasionally adults, stared, pointed fingers, and said "*gaigin*" when they saw us.

The Japanese love their offspring and choose to express their affection by seeming laxity in discipline. Our grandsons Vaughn and Cameron were age seven and five at the time of our visit. Like typical boys, they were naughty at times and, in Western fashion, their parents spanked them. One day Karen spanked Cam (quickly and lightly) when he threw a tantrum in a store. She noticed at once that the Japanese who observed it were obviously very displeased, and she therefore resolved not to lay hands on Cam (in public) again.

We noticed that Japan feels friendly toward Western people. One big reason is that when, at the end of World War II, the conquering forces came marching into the country under General Douglas MacArthur, he gave strict orders that the vanquished foe be given humane treatment. The Japanese were truly amazed, and they have not forgotten to this day.

The people of Japan love to give gifts. We were totally unprepared for the way they lavished gifts upon us. One evening we were invited out to dinner in the Oya home. At the end of the meal, Mrs. Oya gave us five, large, expensive dolls! We were overwhelmed.

Even though the dolls were only a part of the many gifts pressed upon us by the generous Japanese people, we accumulated a total of 19 dolls, including four very large ones in glass cases. Although we filled large cartons and stuffed our suitcases, we were not able to take all of them with us on our return flight.

The food was different, but good. Sitting on the floor at a low Japanese table is very painful to Western bones and muscles. We were awkward, but we managed until we tried to get back on our feet. At that point some of our group (who shall remain nameless) needed assistance.

At one bountiful meal we were served many varieties of Japan's most exotic raw fish preparations. Believe it or not, raw fish is good. It does not taste as "fishy" raw as it does after being cooked. One different dish that evening was barbecued eel. Bob and I found it to be delicious, but the women declined. To them, eel was a bit too much.

Bob and I went shopping one day at a nearby produce store. We noticed that beautiful, ripe tomatoes were priced lower than greener ones. We bought them and saw that the man who waited on us seemed to be amused. Karen told us after we arrived back at the house that Japanese do not like ripe tomatoes. No doubt the man at the store thought we males didn't know what we were doing.

Some Western foods were not available in the Land of the Rising Sun. From childhood Karen always had Wheaties for breakfast. But that was impossible in Japan. So we took her a large box—in our overcrowded suitcase. I saw her eating a carefully measured small serving one morning, and there was a faraway look in her eyes.

We took Dan some M&M candies, and he let it be known that anyone eating his chocolates would suffer dire consequences! We had, of course, taken other candy for the boys.

We learned that education is taken very seriously in Japan. Vaughn and Cam spent five and a half days a week in the classroom each week, eleven months a year. Incredibly, Vaughn had homework during his one-month vacation and needed to report to school two half-days each week.

One result was that the boys became proficient in the language. As we moved about in public places, it was delightful to see the surprised looks on people's faces when Vaughn, the redheaded *gaigin* (foreigner), spoke in fluent Japanese and with the correct local accent.

We all went to DisneyWorld, which had just opened in Tokyo. Everyone had a wonderful time, especially the boys. We could always spot Vaughn, even when he was far away in the crowd. His red head was very easy to find in the sea of otherwise black ones. Mickey Mouse looked the same as he did in the States, but it somehow seemed strange for him to speak in Japanese.

In General Sherman's words, "War is hell." This is true whether in Georgia, at Pearl Harbor, or in Hiroshima. We visited the places marking the beginning and ending of the war with Japan. More than 2,000 American servicemen lost their lives at Pearl Harbor on December 7, 1941. President Roosevelt declared it "a date which will live in infamy." And indeed it has.

We also stood at the site of the big atomic bomb explosion in Hiroshima. A brass plate marks the center of destruction. As we looked at it, we mourned for the 300,000 Japanese of Hiroshima and Nagasaki, at least half of whom were women and children, who died in those blinding flashes and the horrible agony which followed in the next few days.

We visited the Peace Dome and the large Children's Monument. The latter was almost covered with thousands of folded paper crane wreaths, made by children all over Japan. Karen told us that it is always so.

It was a very hot day, and we were most uncomfortable. Then we visited the museum and park which mark the central area of the devastation. We became painfully aware that on another August day the searing heat was so intense it burned stone. As we pondered that fact, the heat we felt was more bearable.

We also noticed that Japanese congregations are small. Dan told us that very few Christian churches in Japan have more than 50 in attendance at their Sunday morning services. Becoming a Christian in Japan is a slow, painful decision. Family and peer pressure are very powerful deterring factors.

What a challenge! What a potential for discouragement. But our missionaries are planning their work and working their plan. We people at home need to constantly support them with our prayers and finances.

When we said goodbye to our four dear ones at the Tokyo Airport, I felt like a deserter because by that time I was much more aware of the painful isolation which they and other missionaries felt. My anguish of separation was deeper than ever; hopefully my prayers became more effective in the days following.

When I first published my feelings about Dan and Karen's going to Japan in the *Evangelical Visitor*, some people let me know that my dedication to God and Christian evangelism left something to be desired. However, many who were among the "sending ones," shared with me that they had experienced the same feelings, but did not have the courage to go public with them.

More than nine years has passed since our visit, and Dan and Karen have settled back into life in the U.S. Since they left Japan, the Nagoya Church has grown, and a new church was built recently.

In the first few years after we returned home, we travelled to quite a number of churches showing the slide-tape presentation I produced at the suggestion of our Board for World Missions.

When I mentioned the slow growth of the Japanese churches, I challenged the various congregations in the U.S. and Canada to show me figures that they had faster "adult conversion growth" than the congregations in Japan. No pastor or layman responded.

It seems evident, does it not, that in countries where we should be winning adult converts with relative ease when compared to the hindrances in Japan, our record is a bit embarrassing.

Surely we will want to join in a mighty prayer effort that more of the dear Japanese people will make the difficult decision to become Christians. And may we people at home put forth greater efforts to win more adults to Christ.

Chapter 15

The Man
We Shouldn't Have Asked

The title of the column I wrote for our church publication in the six years I was employed by the Stewardship Office was "Money Matters." This chapter will include a few of those articles along with items from other sources.

The Man We Shouldn't Have Asked

In the early '50s, when I was the associate pastor of the congregation in Clarence Center, New York, we decided to build an addition to the church. At that time our church was a part of the Canadian Regional Conference.

As was the custom then, we were granted permission to conduct an every-member solicitation of the Canadian Conference churches to raise money for our building fund. Among my contacts was the Wainfleet Congregation. The late Pastor Edward Gilmore, whom I came to love dearly through the years, accompanied me to the various homes of his people.

After we had made quite a number of stops, with good success, he mentioned the name of one brother in the Wainfleet fellowship. "We really shouldn't ask 'Harry' for money—for two reasons. First, he is so poor that his children are ragged and sometimes hungry. And second, he is too generous."

He thought about it for a while as we sat in my car. Finally, reluctantly, he decided to visit Harry. When we arrived, he was outside the house and he hurried over to us. I soon became acquainted with a joyous believer in the midst of obvious poverty.

Pastor Gilmore told him about our Clarence Center project but assured him that it would be perfectly all right if he didn't have any money to spare that day.

Harry hauled out his battered billfold with a flourish and showed the contents to us—a forlorn, two-dollar bill. "That's all I have," he declared, "but I'm going to give it to you." And with the light of heaven radiating from his countenance he offered the rust-colored bill to me. I refused to accept it until Pastor Gilmore whispered that I should.

As I started the car and drove away, I found it hard to focus on the highway. After some moments of silence, I asked why we had accepted the money.

"That question is not easy to answer," he replied slowly. And then he smiled his warm smile. "But you know, Paul, I believe God has just given Harry a very special blessing for his cheerful giving of all he had."

That was almost 40 years ago. But ever since, when I am tempted to feel that increasing my giving to the church is too costly, I get a vision of Harry's two-dollar bill.

"Wing and a Prayer" Challenge!

The big announcement was about to be made. It was Thursday morning, July 10, at the opening of the final session of the 1986 General Conference in Hamilton, Ontario. The moderator presented the general treasurer of the

church. The air was electric with suspense/anticipa-
tion/fear/hope.

As the treasurer made a few preliminary remarks, I
murmured to myself what must have been the strong feeling of the entire conference body and many guests who had
also gathered to hear whether the goal had been achieved.
"Please let us know. This tension is more than I can bear!"

Our treasurer cleared his throat and paused, enjoying
the drama of the event. And then he told us. But first, let me
give you the story from the beginning.

In an earlier session the Board for Evangelism and
Church Planting (BECP) gave their report. We learned that
they had carried out the mandate of the brotherhood and
had planted ten new churches in 1985. As part of their
report, the board asked 14 couples to come forward who
either had begun, or would begin in the near future, church
plantings across North America. Their testimonies and
prayer requests brought excitement and joy, and very natu-
rally led to a prayer of thanksgiving and dedication.

That was the good news. But then came the bad news.

Because contributions for the general fund for out-
reach ministries had fallen short of the approved budget,
the BECP was forced to borrow $150,000 to meet its com-
mitments (mostly for pastoral salaries) in the past year. And
it was forced to drastically reduce the number of churches
to be planted in the current year.

(Why did the board overspend? The chairman and
other young leadership on BECP were eager and a bit ideal-
istic, not being as aware as they should have been that every
year in recent memory it had been necessary to keep spending by boards below the approved budget because of short-
falls.)

During the coffee break on Tuesday morning, I and
two other members of the Commission on Stewardship and
Finance were discussing the problem. One of us, in a Spirit-
inspired moment, suggested that something should be done
about the debt immediately. Looking ahead to the evangelism focus rally the following evening, he said, "Let's find a

few individuals who together will match what the people will give in an offering—up to $50,000. And let's challenge the board to pay off $50,000 on their deficit this year. With everyone working together, we can liquidate the whole debt!"

We three men agreed to try it. Other church administrators were contacted and gave their glad assent. The BECP came on board, fully aware that their fingers were being gently slapped, and also aware that they would need to stretch their resources to the limit to carry out their part of the bargain.

The matching funds persons were found. Everything was in place except informing the Conference body.

The executive director of stewardship in the Canadian Conference presented the challenge to the assembly. He did a superb job, emphasizing that the cash and commitments should not come from regular church budget funds. He urged, "Don't give until it hurts; give until you feel joy!"

The momentum began to build. People were thinking hard and praying for God's guidance. Phone calls were made to spouses and friends. Plans for the purchase of some personal items were abandoned.

The atmosphere was charged with expectancy as the Wednesday evening rally began. When the offering time came, a final challenge was made. The ushers collected the money and faith promises and took their precious cargo away to be counted.

Since it took a long time to tally the results, no announcement was made at the close of the service. It was decided to keep the totals a closely guarded secret until the morning session on Thursday. That wasn't easy; many people urgently wanted to know.

The big moment was finally at hand. The treasurer, smiling broadly, shared the good news—the total was $61,852 in cash and pledges! And more was still coming in.

In the words of the children, who also exceeded their goal of $250 for books and tapes for a children's home, "We blasted our goal!"

Did you ever try to cheer, and cry, and applaud all at the same time? That's what the Conference crowd did in a contemporary version of saying *Halleluhah*! After things quieted down, a hearty prayer of praise was offered.

I fervently wish that every member of the church could have been there. It was a moment to be savored for a lifetime.

Too Young to Give?

Heather was only ten years old in 1987. She was the daughter of pastor of the Ashland, Ohio, church. Her name was not placed on the list of possible givers toward the church's capital fund campaign, with a goal of $125,000. She was, in the careful judgment of considerate people, too young.

She also was not included among those invited to the fellowship dinner, the kick-off event for the fund drive. Ten-year-olds don't enjoy such affairs, the older ones thought.

I agreed, having suggested as consultant that no one under 12 be placed on the lists. Besides, the banquet plates were $10 each. It wouldn't be good stewardship to invite children to the dinner.

As far as I know, Heather didn't raise any objections. But here is what this young miss did. First, she asked to be included in the 24-hour prayer chain that was organized for that final, big weekend as people were making up their minds on the amount of their commitments. When her request was granted, she chose 3:00 a.m. as her time. Three o'clock in the morning!

Her dad was amazed, but tired as he was from all the extra work relating to the campaign, he offered to accompany her to the church. When they arrived, Heather went to the prayer room and her father went to his office. Beyond a doubt, he spent some of the time wondering how long she would last. Well, she remained for the full hour, and she reported that she had a wonderful time! Have you ever prayed for a solid hour?

Heather's second move was to ask for a commitment

card. She filled it in carefully—for 25 cents a week, for 150 weeks, a total of $37.50. And she committed herself to two other responsibilities: to pray regularly for her church, and to give weekly to the annual budget needs (as she had been doing). Then she neatly signed her name: *Heather R. Engle.*

To his credit, the general chairman of the campaign made an appointment with her to pick up the commitment card. It was to be placed in a sealed envelope, like all the others. When he arrived, Mrs. Engle handed him the envelope with the explanation that Heather was playing with a friend and didn't have time to see him. Isn't it delightful to discover that she was, after all, a child?

What is it that causes a little girl to pray, and give, and make a commitment for 150 consecutive weeks? One can never be sure, but a contributing factor may have been that her father and mother decided to make a three-year commitment of $10,000 to the fund drive, and they volunteered to announce their decision from the pulpit a week before other people of the congregation made their commitments.

I suppose we shouldn't be all that amazed to learn that the commitments by the Ashland people (only 56 members) surpassed the $150,000 mark, well beyond the goal. And I suppose that none of us should be surprised that Heather is the kind of person she is.

It happens that her commitment was the smallest one turned in. That is, in the eyes of people. In the eyes of God, in combination with her 60-minute prayer, it could well be among the largest.

Too Old to Give?

Mrs. "Smith" was in her eighties. For many years she had served faithfully as a pastor's wife, pouring out her life in devotion to her family and the church. She had been a widow for more than 15 years.

While she was still in her seventies it seemed like she could no longer keep her accounts straight. Money was being used up, and she often had no idea where it had gone. Her children were exasperated.

A television preacher made her an offer that was too good to refuse. He said that he had a large family Bible that was worth more than $50, and that it would be given as a gift to anyone who gave the broadcast a gift of $25. Mrs. Smith had nine children, and so she sent the preacher $225—for nine Bibles.

At Christmas time she proudly gave each of her children one of the large Bibles.

"Mother!" they exclaimed in dismay, "Where did you get all those Bibles?"

And so she explained what a bargain they had been. The children did their best to appear thankful, but they were unhappy with what Mother had done, partly because they were not enthused about the television preacher she was supporting.

Because of those gifts and others like them, and because she was frequently out of money and genuinely puzzled as to how it had been spent, the children asked two of their siblings to help manage her money. With that arrangement, her financial affairs worked out better, and she seemed to be much relieved.

One evening there was a fund-raising dinner for a religious charity of which the children approved. Her oldest son "Jim" invited her to go along, just to relieve her boredom. She gladly consented.

The meals were free. After the food had been served, a heart-stirring appeal was made, with testimonials of how people had been greatly helped by the ministry. It was clearly evident that people were going to respond.

Opportunity was given for cash offerings and commitments to be paid at a later date. A fervent prayer was offered, asking God to direct the givers. The people began to fill in their cards.

Mrs. Smith leaned toward her son. "Is it all right, James, for me to make a donation?"

Jim was dubious. "How much do you want to give, Mother?" She could tell he was not happy about her request.

"I would like to give all I have in my purse," she ventured timidly.

Her son frowned. "And how much is that?"

"Two dollars."

He nodded his approval, a bit reluctantly.

His mother carefully filled out the card, put it into an envelope along with the two dollars, and handed the envelope to an usher collecting them.

The procedure at that meeting was to have the chairman open the envelopes and call out the amounts. A secretary with a calculator kept a running total. Gifts ranged anywhere from a thousand dollars to twenty-five dollars.

And then the chairman looked at a card and paused. Jim was watching him. It seemed to him that he was ready to call out two hundred dollars, and then caught himself just in time when he saw the decimal point. Two dollars, he announced rather quietly. Everything was quiet. One could almost see the wheels of people's minds turning. "Who is the deadbeat who has just eaten a twelve dollar dinner and has given only a two dollar donation?" (The son had given a generous gift, easily enough to represent both himself and his mother.)

As the people went home, they must surely have remembered both the thousand dollar gift and the two dollar gift. It seems to me that Jesus once called the attention of his disciples to a similar offering.

Trash Can Collection

Did you ever see a garbage container used to receive an offering? I didn't either until one Sunday some months ago.

A pastor in Pennsylvania received a sample bank from Campus Crusade for Christ. It was round and plastic, and it caught his attention. Campus Crusade said they would supply enough banks for all his families and 60 percent of the proceeds could remain in the local church.

The congregation, picking up their pastor's suggestion, decided to give it a try. A good supply of the banks were ordered (at no cost) and nearly all were taken by interested families and individuals. A date was chosen for Shake Out Sunday! and it was announced that the local proportion would go to world missions.

The pastor wasn't sure what the response would be, since the giving to the regular offerings continued to come in well. He need not have feared. As the date approached, the big banks became fuller and fuller.

On Shake Out Sunday! he placed a large new plastic trash can at the front of the sanctuary (obscuring the communion table!) with a poster attached making it clear that "This is for the Shake Out offering." The table beside it was quickly filled with the loaded banks as people arrived for the morning service. In fact, the response was so good that some of the banks spilled over on the floor.

I happened to be the speaker that October morning, telling stories about how "God Is Working through our Ministries." When the children were asked to come forward to shake the contents of the banks into the trash container, I could not resist the excitement, so I went to the scene of the action and noise. What a commotion for the Lord!

My hope was that someone would give me a bank and let me join the shakers, but I wished even more for a camera. Going to the microphone, I begged for someone to bring a camera forward. No cameras were attending church that morning—perhaps I was not heard above the din.

The pastor found an offering envelope among the banks. After he had reduced the noise level to the communication level, he held up the envelope and announced that it contained $260! He discovered later that he had given the envelope number by mistake. It was that kind of morning.

More and more coins and folding money were shaken into the trash container, and it became heavier and heavier. When the pastor tried to lift it, he almost threw his shoulders out of joint. Well, at any rate, he asked people not to lift it after the service for fear of breaking the handles. It was his own trash can, just recently purchased.

When the last coin hit the top of the pile, the pastor

enthused, "This has been a noisy clanging praise! All this money will be used to share the gospel of Jesus with others all over the world."

The Shake Out was later followed by a weigh-in. That morning the weight came to 116 pounds and the cash amounted to $946.21. When more banks were brought in later, the total weight reached 136 pounds and the total offering came to $1,141.30.

What an exhilarating experience. The children loved it. The rest of us did too. In the pastor's words, "It's wonderful to help people catch the vision of giving joyfully to worthwhile causes. Giving to our general ministries is showing itself over and over to be of great value to the whole church, and we all need to give them our best support." Amen!

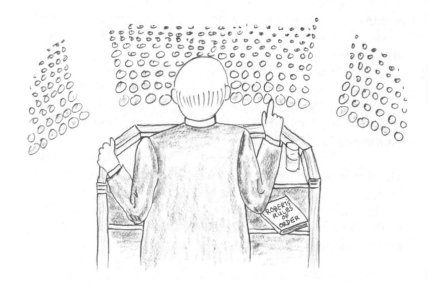

Chapter 16

Convention Fun and Folly

The North American assembly of our church is looked forward to with high anticipation by young and old. It is a combination of business, inspirational meetings and other activities for all age groups, ample time for fellowship, and good meals.

For many it is the high point of the church life cycle. That is my own attitude as well.

My father loved to attend this annual event, and I have inherited his high regard for our great convocation. My wife Lela and our children share this deep feeling.

My parents took me to my first church-wide conference in 1934, when I was nine years old. The site was a beautiful campground in Ludlow Falls, Ohio. The great occasion was a time of freedom and fun, of attending children's meetings, of playing games, of eating ice cream and candy (Dad was always in a more expansive mood). I dashed about the tents and trees with newly-found friends. Some of those friendships have lasted through the years.

The next year we three oldest boys of the family travelled with Dad and Mother to a church north of Toronto, Ontario, for the big convocation. It was my first trip across an international border, and I noticed the skinny-tired bicycles, the different flag, and a more clipped accent.

Lela Swalm, my wife of the future, was there, but she didn't notice this 10-year-old lad from "the States," as the Canadians put it. She, after all, was almost two years older and practically a teenager. Her attention, and that of the girls she was running around with, was on the handsome young men of the male quartets from Messiah and Upland Colleges.

I also attended a later conference in Canada, at a church near Fort Erie, Ontario. The year was 1942, and I had become interested in the fairer sex. However, my attentions were given to a young lady from Ohio, also there. My heart ached when she spurned me in favor of another young man attending.

Lela was again there, but again she didn't notice me because she was dating another fellow. By that time she was all of 19. Of course, I failed to notice her as well. I returned home feeling rejected.

We were both at the conference in 1949, held at a campground in Stayner, Ontario, near Lela's home church. This was the year of our August wedding. Lela was actively involved in the information booth, and I "assisted" her. That conference is notable as the time when a disputed nominating committee report had the weary delegates wrestling with a final decision long after midnight.

I missed the gathering of 1950 because Beth, our first daughter, was born on July 9. She was the first grandchild on both sides, and both sets of grandparents thought she was a "wonder to behold."

My 40-year record of consecutive General Conference attendance began in 1951, when the large group convened at Manhattan, Kansas. One over-riding memory of that convention was the weather—it rained almost without ceasing.

All the rain gear in town was sold out before I arrived. I ruined my best pair of shoes as I slogged around in the mud. The day after the convention ended, the whole campground was under water!

It has been my privilege to share in various areas of service at the denominational level. My first such appointment was as a member of the newly-created Commission on Radio at that Manhattan meeting.

At one such convention near West Milton, Ohio, a hotly-debated question was on the floor. The final speaker before the vote was a skilled communicator. When he spoke, *everyone* knew exactly where he stood on the matter being discussed. After he completed his compelling speech, the moderator called for the vote.

But just as he was doing so, a delegate jumped to his feet. Now, this man was noted for being a bit confused at times. He raised a question which was unthinkably out of place. "Brother Moderator," he stammered, "what I want to know before we vote is—on which side of the question was the last speaker speaking?" There was a moment of stunned silence, and then the delegates broke into prolonged laughter.

After the sound subsided, the speaker rose to his feet. "It was my intention," he smilingly told the questioner, "to speak in favor of the question." With that word, the vote was taken, and the motion passed with a strong response. The inquiring brother was even informed enough to vote for it. Of course, it could have been that he intended to vote against it!

At a later convention I referred to this incident and then went on to debate the issue at hand. The next speaker, referring to my story, stated that he, ironically, was finding it hard to determine which side of the issue I was supporting. Touche!

At our annual meeting at the Roxbury Camp there was a rather pronounced thump during a quiet moment of a business session. Someone had fallen off the end of a bench. A doctor hurried over to give assistance. Before long the man, a minister from Michigan, was restored to his seat. His face was very red, and there was a lump on the side of his head. He had simply fallen asleep and tumbled from his seat onto the concrete floor.

At still another conference, the speaker in an evening inspirational session was holding forth on "Reaching New Frontiers." There was just one problem—he pronounced the final word "front-ears." He waxed eloquent on all kinds of promising and challenging front-ears.

More and more people began to be amused with his description of the demanding front-ears of the brotherhood! Even the gentle, dignified, always proper conference secretary, began to laugh. His embarrassment was obvious to many who sat near him. Even today I can picture that meeting, with the preacher very serious in his plea that we move forward to ever more extended front-ears! And I can envision, once again, the many uncomfortable people who did their best to conceal their laughter.

At another such meeting at Azusa Pacific University I was making announcements at the close of the session in connection with my responsibilities as convention director. The night before, my wife and I had been disturbed at a very late hour by some youths engaged in loud conversation on the sidewalk near our window. I resolved to do something about it.

I told the conference members about the group of teenagers. One of them, I stated, had talked with unusual volume and length. I told the delegates, "I am very sorry that it is necessary to name the teenager, but it seems to me that an example should be made of him."

I looked at the moderator and the secretary. They looked unhappy. I looked at the assembly. "Surely," their faces told me, "you won't do this to one of our teenagers."

I told them again that I wouldn't name the teenager unless I considered it absolutely necessary. But I could tell that the crowd was praying silently that I wouldn't do it.

I paused, taking a deep breath. "The teenager," I declared, "was none other than our denominational editor!"

The whole conference body was so relieved, and so amused, that they exploded with applause! It went on and on as they vented their delight with the announcement.

After things finally quieted down, the conference secretary called out in a stentorian voice, *"Will our editor please come forward."*

As he made his way to the platform the delegates applauded again. I can see him yet, standing there with a red face.

"I am pleased to inform you," he announced, "that your ovation was the strongest I have ever received!"

And then he turned to me, "I am willing to forgive you, Paul, for your accusation only because you have included me with the teenagers!" He then went on to announce the distribution of the conference issue of the *Evangelical Visitor,* a tradition of many years' standing. (By the way, the editor had actually been talking to a group of teenagers outside our window. They had arrived late at night and he was giving them directions to their rooms, loud and clear.)

At another conference in California, a carload of delegates skipped a day of sessions and went to Disneyland. The moderator learned about the escapade and decided "to put those men in their place."

The next morning he addressed the assembly. "I have learned," he stated very solemnly, "that a carload of delegates played hooky and went to Disneyland yesterday. That was a most despicable thing to do. Your congregations," he told them, "spent a lot of hard-earned money to send you across the continent to this important meeting. You should be ashamed of yourselves!"

Everyone looked around to see who the offenders were. The objects of the scolding did their best to look innocent. The whole crowd of attenders (many of whom had also wanted to attend Disneyland, I suspect) very much enjoyed the verbal punishment being administered.

With many other words did the moderator exhort the errant brethren to mend their ways. His sarcasm was a wonder to behold. He was well known by almost all the delegates. They therefore knew that he was very serious about the matter. They also knew that he was having a lot of fun applying the verbal scourge!

As for the men involved, although I never knew who they were, I was told, by someone who can usually be trusted, that they mended their ways—the following day they went to Knotts Berry Farm, but only during the afternoon session!

At one annual gathering a young teen was given the job of collecting meal tickets at the dining room door. "Under no circumstances," he was instructed, "should you allow anyone to enter the dining room without a ticket."

He was duly impressed.

One day the conference moderator came to the dining room. He fumbled around for his ticket, but couldn't find it. He was in a hurry, with only about 15 minutes before his next appointment. He told the young ticket collector who he was and what office he held, and that he would bring him a ticket later.

But the lad hung in there! "Sorry, you will have to get a ticket!"

The moderator later commended him. Both greatly enjoyed telling the story.

The temperatures ran very high at one conference held at Messiah College. I happened to be working on the platform as recording secretary that year. The delegates were sitting on old folding chairs, with dark stain-varnish on the backs (made of V-jointed boards). During the course of the session, the perspiring delegates took off their suit jackets.

At the close of the session, as they turned around, they first saw the dark brown stripes on the shirts of fellow-delegates, and then they suddenly realized that their own shirts also had streaks on them!

The college administrators were embarrassed. Before another such gathering was convened, they had all the seats refinished.

Almost from the beginning, the general convocation has been composed of all the congregations from both Canada and the United States. There has always been a lot of good natured ribbing about the disadvantages of being a Canadian or an American.

At a convention at Messiah College, a Canadian got up and, with sober face and voice, expressed his deep regret that he had found clear signs of racial discrimination on the campus. He labored the point so much that I noticed the college president becoming very concerned. He leaned forward to better see and hear the speaker.

With a very straight face the Canadian explained. "I went to get myself a can of soda from a dispensing machine, and a big sign on the machine said 'Do NOT use Canadian Coins in this Machine.' I feel deeply offended indeed."

The president relaxed and laughed with the others. I later saw someone seated near the unhappy Canadian offer him something. Very possibly it was American money. I hope he was mollified.

Chapter 17

Another "Littlest Angel"

The longer I live, the more I'm convinced that memorial services for Christians are times of celebration. This is true even when the circumstances surrounding physical death seem to be sad and even tragic. Such sorrow and grieving, however, are for the ones who remain, not for the one who has gone to be with the Lord.

I have attended quite a number of funerals through the years. From these, I have selected four to write about—a child, a teenager, a mature man, and a woman in her late eighties.

Another "Littlest Angel"

One of my first pastoral calls after beginning to serve the congregation in Grantham, Pennsylvania, was in the home of Ron and Shirley Brubaker. At the time these fine Christian parents had two daughters, Jodi and Vicki, and a son of about five months.

Little Chad was a "special child," to use the familiar euphemism. His characteristic features of Down's Syndrome were clearly evident to my wife and me.

Ron and Shirley were very open in discussing their challenging circumstance with us. The serene smile on Shirley's face was beautiful to behold, even when tears started chasing each other down her cheeks. Ah, the agonies and ecstasies of parenthood. But only parents of special children can understand this particular dimension fully.

Pastors try, but they often fall short. I felt most inadequate that evening. How wonderful that our Lord, who is "a man of sorrows and acquainted with grief," brought comfort to the Brubakers then and in the days following.

About six years later Chad contracted a severe respiratory infection. His mother took him to the doctor. That evening at home he continued to breathe with difficulty. And then, he just stopped breathing. The little memorial card at his funeral stated that he "entered into rest, December 30, 1975."

Chad was such an affectionate child. Long after other children were "making strange" he continued to give his love recklessly to all.

And he was so obviously a happy child. The cheery disposition of his early years and his It's-wonderful-to-be-alive! outlook on life stayed with him all his days. With the Grantham people, Chad was indeed a very special person.

One wonders if it is a God-directed irony or a fallen-nature fact that "normal" children soon learn to reserve their affection for a very limited number of people, and that children with average intelligence soon learn to frown more and smile less.

One of his teachers at the Grantham Church was among the many recipients of Chad's love. And she had a special compartment of love in her heart for the little lad. On her way home from his funeral she stopped in a bookstore and purchased two copies of *The Littlest Angel*, an enchanting Christmas story.

She gave one to the church library in Chad's memory and gave the other to his parents. Since the book happens to be my favorite Christmas story (other than the Bible accounts), the teacher's thoughtful gesture impressed me as being one of the most thoroughly just-right happenings in a long time.

The Littlest Angel, like Chad in many ways, found himself in heaven one day. Because he was doing all kinds of impetuous things, he frequently managed to ruffle the feathers of dignified "normal" angels. Unfortunately, he didn't seem to improve as eternity went on.

After the Littlest Angel had scampered on the golden streets for what seemed like a very long time to him, the date approached in God's plan for Jesus to be born in the Bethlehem manger. All the angels rejoiced, and each one began to prepare a gift for the Christ-child. But the Littlest Angel had a big problem in that his artistic skills, like his behavior, left something to be desired. He prayed a whole series of "panic prayers."

When the day came for presenting the gifts before the throne of the Almighty God, the downcast cherub held only a small rough box which he had brought from earth. All heaven held its breath as God opened the box and beheld butterfly wings, a sky-blue bird's egg, two white stones, and an old dog collar—which the Littlest Angel had salvaged from the neck of his faithful mongrel, who died as he had lived, with boundless love and utter devotion.

God, to the great surprise of the heavenly host, was pleased. In fact, he liked that gift better than all the more imposing gifts of thousands of other angels. Then something wonderful happened! But then, you will want to read the book for yourself, and share the story with a wide-eyed child.

As for Chad, he is now forever delivered from the limitations of mind and body. For Ron and Shirley Brubaker there is a new kind of agony and ecstasy. But for the new Littlest Angel, only ecstasy.

Summa Cum Laude*

During one of the years we were living on the campus of Messiah College, Eunice Metzler, a Mennonite girl from Manheim, Pennsylvania, was attending classes. She was a hard-working student and an earnest Christian, the kind of person the college is always proud to have enrolled.

But in January this bonnie lass of 19 years died following open-heart surgery. All her life she lived under the shadow of a heart that threatened to stop its labored beating. When she was four years old the doctor predicted that she probably wouldn't live past the age of seven.

And so she lived life intensely, buying up the moments as treasured jewels. Her parents recalled that even as a small child she talked much about heaven. It comes as no surprise then that she accepted Christ as her Savior at age ten.

Eunice had her first open-heart operation when she was 16. Her fearlessness in facing the surgeon's knife then, and again just before her death, spoke to and challenged many people. Her theme verse was "The eternal God is thy refuge; underneath are the everlasting arms" (Deut. 33:27).

She had beautiful dark eyes which glowed as focal lights in the setting of a wistful face. My only encounter with her was in a small prayer group not many weeks before she died. I didn't know she was ill then; I only noted that she talked lovingly of her Lord and that her fellow students gave careful attention when she spoke.

She, like many other girls, shared her thoughts with her diary. On the day of her funeral some of these were shared with her friends. Her words ministered to me:

As I look forward to the future, I am able to face it with eagerness and anticipation, for I know Christ will

---

* *Summa Cum Laude* is used in connection with diplomas granted to outstanding graduates and means "with highest distinction."

go with me. His grace is sufficient for me. I don't have the least inkling what the future holds for me, but that will be all the more exciting. I'm sure the previous chapters in my life have been a means of preparing me for future chapters. When will my life end? I don't know that either. But there's nothing to be frightened about, for I'm sure my Author will finish it at the right moment.... And so I close this chapter of my life with a smile and tears; eager to face the future and yet sentimental about leaving the things which have helped me arrive where I am.

One entry is a prayer.

Thank you, Lord, for the quiet moments which I can have every evening before going to bed. It is so refreshing, these moments with You. May I sleep well tonight and awake with great anticipation for a new day.

And finally, this confession:

God, I can't see You tonight; the cloud is too big, too dark. But I know You are there. And I hear You saying, "Wait on the Lord; be of good courage and He shall strengthen thy heart. Wait, I say, on the Lord." And so I'll wait because someday, someday soon, I'll penetrate that cloud and fly to realms beyond it.

And that is exactly what she did!

At this point I can hear some sophisticated teens (and older ones too) say, "Come off all that sentimental stuff. Tell it like it is. Face the harsh facts. Eunice is dead, and she would rather be living, and we want her back."

Of course Eunice is dead. I said so in the third sentence of this article. And the human in me is also resentful that she died so young, and scared because my own life guarantee is just as uncertain.

But her testimony is for real. You can search our world, and our universe, for a better way to live and a more confident way to die, and you will come up empty-handed.

I choose to stake my life and hopes with Eunice who declared, "...someday soon, I'll penetrate that cloud and fly to realms beyond it!" You and I can fully agree with Eunice and also with the Apostle Paul who joyfully proclaimed, "For me to live is Christ; to die is gain."

He Was a Brother Beloved

I had just returned from a funeral some years ago and felt impelled to share some feelings which went through my mind during the service.

Pastor Ralph Palmer (I wrote) was felled a few days ago by the combined forces of diabetes and kidney failure. He was a tall tree in our forest, and there is now a large empty space against the sky. Because he was barely forty-two years old, his home-going seems truly tragic.

But the service was a celebration. All the music and spoken words had notes of victory and hope. When the young widow, Esther, came in she was wearing a beautiful white cape, and the words "like a bride adorned for her husband" flashed through my mind. Ralph Jr., a tall high school senior standing at his mother's side, was wearing a bright red jacket. And I thought—what a fitting way for people to dress even at a funeral when they believe that a loved one's dying day is his coronation day.

In the moments before the service started my mind wandered back across a couple decades. Ralph was enrolled at Messiah College in the early 1950s. He was just getting started as a young preacher in those days, and consented to serve as assistant pastor at Rana Villa, a small community church I was pastoring about five miles away.

It is not hard to remember the first sermon he preached there. His text was "Ye must be born again." He stressed the absolute MUST of the new birth until no one in that service could possibly have missed the point of his eloquent plea and warning. Would that this were characteristic of more sermons.

Some time later Ralph became so discouraged with his college experience and preaching potential that he was tempted to quit one or the other, or both. With downcast eyes he told me. When I urged him to renew his efforts, he did so and came through "on a wing and a prayer." Actually, this had slipped from my memory until Esther told me as we stood beside the open casket.

He was a brother beloved.

Like many others, he was hard pressed for funds during his college days. One source of income was preaching for revival meetings in small churches. During the course of such a meeting, he related how the Lord had helped him drive home a point in his sermon the night before.

He was preaching on eternal punishment. Just as he was stressing the scriptural truth regarding hell fire, all the lights went out. It was winter time and the central heating system was a pot-bellied stove in the center of the room. The stove door was open and, as Ralph told it, the hearers were "really impressed" with the bright flicker of the flames and the reflections they cast on the walls. I can still see the flash of his eyes as he drew that word picture.

Yes, he was a brother beloved.

In those years he was struggling with the painful problem of theological differences with the denomination of which he was then a member. He had become deeply convinced of the teachings of the Brethren in Christ, and some leaders of his own denomination could not accept such doctrines in their circles. Only those who have been forced to such a parting of the ways by their own deep convictions can know the heartache connected with Ralph's decision to join another fellowship.

Is there any wonder that in the tributes given at the funeral were such words as "strong holiness concern . . . anointed of the Spirit . . . compassion . . . sincerity and fervor . . . one of God's choice servants . . . loved to preach the Word . . . pastor's heart . . . shepherd"?

Ralph was serving as the pastor of the Mechanicsburg Church at the time of his death. His bishop, Dr. Henry A. Ginder, told me tearfully that becoming reconciled to Ralph's passing was one of the most difficult experiences of his life.

It seems to me that Ralph's death was as untimely in our eyes as the death of Stephen, another bold young preacher in New Testament times. But that tragedy and triumph of long ago helped produce the great Apostle Paul.

I thank God for the memory of my brother beloved and pray that the tragedy and triumph of his departure will bring forward other fearless preachers of the Word.

The final funeral story of the chapter is one by Beth Hostetler Mark, about her Grandmother Swalm.

Eighties the Best Ever!

"Wait 'til you get to the eighties; they're the best ever!" Maggie once told a complaining middle-aged woman. Could this nearly blind, crippled, snowy-haired lady possibly be serious?

As a mother of four, and wife of a traveling evangelist, Maggie Swalm worked hard. Managing the hired hands, cooking for threshing crews, sewing the children's clothes, and doing chores were only a part of her busy life. And she thrived on it.

But now, in her eighties, Maggie could really take time to do what she enjoyed. Unfortunately, failing eyesight ruled out her favorite hobbies of quilting and reading. And her husband could no longer drive—so there she sat in her rocking chair, a perfect candidate for grumbling old womanhood.

In her rural neighborhood she heard rumors of younger women getting together for coffee hours, and she became intrigued with the idea. Lack of transportation did not dissuade her. Picking up the receiver one winter morning she telephoned another housebound woman declaring, "Hello, Annie?" Go get yourself a cup of coffee, we're going to have a coffee hour like the young women do!" And they did.

No modern convenience has had better use than the plain black telephone beside Maggie's rocker. Receiver in hand, she regularly communicated with lonely people, young and old, connecting them with something good in the world. The church supplied her with monthly lists of people's birthdays. She tried to call each one on his or her birthday, and more than once the surprised recipients heard her strong soprano voice singing, "Happy Birthday to You!"

The Stayner Church in Ontario, Canada, was Maggie's social as well as spiritual outlet, and it took something major to keep her home on Sundays or Wednesday nights. The last time I visited her she leaned heavily on my arm and her cane, and waded through eight inches of freshly fallen snow to get to prayer meeting.

After services Maggie sat in her front row pew waiting for the church to empty. But she was never alone for long. Children and young people came to her to be teased and to exchange the latest jokes and riddles. At age 89 she kept young children spellbound with her tricks and stories.

Visiting family members were often met with requests to take her to visit hospitalized people or nursing home residents. Dorothy, a much younger woman bedridden with rheumatoid arthritis, always responded with a smile when Maggie came to see her.

Maggie was accustomed to keeping her hands busy, so she began to knit afghans and lap robes, which did not demand sharp eyesight. By the time she reached 89 she had knit close to 100 afghans for friends, the elderly, children, and grandchildren. A few weeks before her death she was trying to finish one for one of her great granddaughters.

Nor did her handicaps keep her from travelling. When forced to use a wheelchair at airports, Maggie didn't protest—she enjoyed having a chauffeur.

The highlight of her later years was an annual trip to Camp Kahquah for the Senior Citizens' Retreat. Though not a public speaker, she loved to perform at the retreat's talent night, often winning first prize. Her own children were astonished to hear that, at the age of 88, she won a prize for playing the harmonica. (They didn't even know she could play!)

Because she didn't consider herself handicapped, God

was able to use Maggie to minister to all ages, with a special gift for relating to young mothers. Of course, she never would have proclaimed such a thing. One of Maggie's daughters once said, "Her life spoke more loudly to me than all the ministers put together." The following letter, written by a young mother 50 years her junior, gives evidence to the fruits of Maggie's ministry.

Dear Maggie:

At noon-time today, as I was putting on my apron, I thought of you again. My two most favorite aprons are the ones you gave me—the full-length ones with the bibs. I wear them all the time and appreciate them so much.

I then started thinking about our many trips in the car together—you and I in the back seat, with E.J. [Bishop Swalm] and Garth in the front seat. [Garth and Jane frequently provided transportation for the Swalms.] I remember how you used to bring along poems and little word games to do, to help pass the time. I also remember how you were so good at amusing the children and keeping them happy—by telling them stories, reading them books, and sharing your riddles with us.

I often would ask you questions about raising children, for I longed for the advice and wisdom of someone whom I trusted and cared for. I believe God gave you to me to help me. You probably don't realize how you have fulfilled Titus 2:3-5 for me.

Truly you, Maggie, as an older woman, have been a teacher of good things. You have taught me more about loving my husband, Garth, and loving our children, Graham and Ian. You have helped me to understand the importance of the qualities Titus mentions in verse 5. I thank you.

You are a dear friend, Maggie, to us all. Our thoughts and prayers are with you.

Keep smiling! The twinkle in your eye and your sense of humor have always blessed me (and many others).

With love,

Jane

In her last weeks, suffering from the gnawing pain of a large cancerous growth, Maggie found yet another group of people who needed her help—her husband and children. For all of their lives they had felt uncomfortable in the presence of death. Now Maggie became their teacher as she accepted with good grace the end of her life on earth. When she was finally forced to spend all her time in bed, she joked about being "as lazy as a pet coon."

She did not long for death, but neither did she fight it. On her last day, Palm Sunday, family members wandered in and out of her room, not wanting to be far from her. Then, in the afternoon, with her husband holding her hand, her children and their spouses, a granddaughter, and a great granddaughter surrounding her, she quietly died.

It was only later, as they lingered in the room, that her children realized they were no longer afraid.

As a lunch was being served after the funeral, I glanced out the window, and I was appalled to see several children running and jumping on the freshly mounded grave. But then I smiled, imagining Grandma's delight that even at her funeral the children were having fun.

Chapter 18

Long Walk Toward Hope

During the course of my years in the ministry, I have preached many sermons. This was especially necessary in my first 20 years of pastoral service, when I usually preached on both Sunday mornings and evenings, and then for the midweek service. It therefore seems appropriate to include a sermon in this book.

But before doing that, let me tell you of a time when my sermon plans went "aglee," as Bobby Burns was wont to say.

In a Christmas sermon at the Grantham Church, my hope was to climax the message with a bit of drama, involving the choir. Before the choir moved into the choir loft that morning, I explained my procedure. I was a bit concerned because two men in the choir didn't seem to be paying proper attention.

At the conclusion of the sermon, I was making the point that if we really believed the Christmas story, it would change our ordinary lives into ones of inspiration and excitement—that one person could make a big difference.

I then walked to the piano and played the descending notes—*do ti la so fa mi re do,* telling the congregation that they were listening to very mundane, uninspired music. But, I declared, "Here is what happens when a master plays those same notes!"

At that point the choir burst forth with the first line of "Joy to the World! the Lord is come; . . ." The effect was breathtaking. It was positively perfect—for about a quarter of a second. The two men who hadn't been paying attention when the instructions were being given (the choir was asked to sing only that first line) sang lustily on with the next line—"let earth recei . . . . "—and then stopped.

There was an embarrassing silence, followed by a few nervous titters. I walked back to the pulpit to bring the sermon to the grand conclusion—a conclusion totally shattered by the unasked-for male duet. I mumbled a few words and then made my escape with a rather hurried benediction.

And so, as someone has aptly put it, the sermon "ended with a whimper rather than a bang."

My only consolation was that the other choir members mercilessly castigated the errant singers for ruining what would have been a great moment for both the choir and the minister. The men were contrite, and they apologized to me, but I suspect they will never live their blunder down. And I also suspect that they are paying more attention when directions are given.

Things went better with my Easter sermon. Learning that the choir was preparing a short cantata on the Bible story of the disciples on the road to Emmaus, I decided to build a "rather different" sermon around that theme.

As it turned out, the choir sang part of the cantata and

I gave about half of the message. The choir then sang the remainder of their music, after which I concluded the sermon. As you will see, it was in the format of a letter written to St. Luke, who was the only gospel writer to record the account.

Emmaus, Judea
One week after Passover
In the year 33 A.D.
To the Physician, Lucas
City of Antioch
Syria

My Beloved Friend Luke:

Grace to you and SHALOM be multiplied!

Since you told me when I last visited in your home that you had some interest in writing a book about the life of Jesus, and since it was not your fortune to be in Jerusalem during the last two weeks, I would like to include some of the terrible and wonderful events of those days in this letter.

I should really give the credit to my wife, Mary, who just a little while ago said, "Cleopas, I am sure that Luke would be very pleased to hear from us about the recent happenings, and especially what happened one week ago as we walked home from Jerusalem." So, here I am, writing to you.

You may find some of these things hard to believe, but that won't bother us. We still find it hard to believe we weren't dreaming at least a part of the recent happenings.

Little did Mary and I know when we moved from Alexandria to our little hot-baths village of Emmaus that we, as devout Jews, would become involved in following a carpenter from Nazareth (of all places) around the countryside. Word was spreading that he had many deep things to say as he went about healing both people's minds and bodies. There were even reports that he cast devils out of tortured victims and once raised a widow's son from the dead as the funeral procession was on its way to the tomb near the village of Nain.

Mary and I had heard about this Jesus of Nazareth for some months before we finally went to hear him in person. I shall never forget the first time he looked into my eyes and quietly asked me to become a part of his kingdom. I held back for quite a while because I wanted to learn what this man from the north country was trying to accomplish.

But after we witnessed the many powerful things he said and did, we became convinced that he was what he claimed to be—the Messiah of whom our prophets had spoken for centuries. The Messiah who would redeem Israel.

And so we decided to cast our lot with him, confident that he had enough power to overthrow our Roman oppressors. Mary and I often talked of the coming glad day when we would put the Romans under the yoke the way they make us bow the neck today.

Two weeks ago it seemed sure that the time had come—that the Nazarene would bring about the revolution and that we Jews would have ourselves a king like David or Solomon. The great Passover feast time was nearing, and thousands of people were either in Jerusalem or coming to Jerusalem. When Jesus and his chosen band of twelve disciples approached the city by way of Bethany and the Mount of Olives, he gave the order for a donkey to be brought to him.

After he mounted the donkey he started down the slope toward our holy city. Many people, remembering the familiar prophecy of a great King to come riding on a donkey, quickly made the association, and the whole multitude of disciples began to rejoice and praise God with a loud voice for all the mighty works they had seen, saying, "Blessed be the King that cometh in the name of the Lord." I was wearing my best cloak, but I took it off and threw it down in front of the little donkey along with many others. Mary got a palm branch and waved it, and we shouted with the people, "Hosanna in the highest!"

What a day it was! Jesus and a large host of us followers went right through the Eastern Gate to the temple. As soon as we arrived, Jesus drove out the cheating money-changers and upset their tables! He then healed many blind and lame men and women. The Kingdom was *his*, and *ours*!

But then he disappointed us all—right at the moment he could have claimed the whole city—by leaving and going back to Bethany to the house of Lazarus and his sisters, Mary and Martha.

During the next three days he seemed satisfied with talking with us and many others who gathered around him. The Master talked about the kind of people who would be a part of his kingdom. How impatient we were to have him make his move and really start acting like the powerful Messiah and King we knew him to be.

Then, about ten days ago, the forces of evil struck. On Thursday night Judas, one of his disciples, betrayed Jesus by kissing him in the presence of the priests and scribes. They had determined to kill him because of their jealousy when so many people left them and their dead traditions and followed this man who dared to call himself the Son of God. After mistreating him harshly for most of the night, they took him before Pilate the next morning and asked for his crucifixion.

Pilate couldn't find anything wrong with him and told the priests that Jesus should be released. But when they threatened to report him to Caesar, the coward washed his hands before us all and turned Jesus over to be crucified.

The whole thing seemed like a dreadful nightmare to Mary and me. We knew that our miracle worker could escape the hateful throng just as he had done once in Galilee when a mob tried to throw him over a cliff.

Then someone near me claimed that he had seen me with Jesus a number of times. That really scared me. Even though I am ashamed to admit it, Luke, I, along with all the men who had been followers of Jesus (except John) went into hiding because we expected to be arrested at any moment. I will never forget the note of reproach in Mary's voice as she said, "Come, Cleopas, let's not leave our Lord when he is in deep trouble."

But I fled while she and some of the other women followed Jesus to the place of the skull outside Jerusalem where the Roman soldiers nailed him to a cross and hung him up between two thieves.

Mary saw him hang there. She saw him in anguish there. She saw him die there. And even though Jesus was obviously dead, a soldier rammed a spear into his heart. Just before sundown Mary saw Joseph and Nicodemus take the body from the cross and lay it in a new tomb nearby. And that was that. The Master was dead. We observed the Sabbath in all the proper ways, but our hearts were like stone.

Then on the first day of the week, just seven days ago, reports started to circulate that someone had stolen the body of Jesus. The rumor started to make its rounds that Jesus was alive again. And with that, Mary and I felt that we could take no more. So about two hours before sundown we slipped away and started the seven-mile trip back home. The dust had never seemed more irritating and the stones sharper than they did that evening. The miles dragged slowly on.

As we walked, Mary and I discussed carefully what had happened. Had we been mistaken about who Jesus was? Would God let such a person die in the way Mary had seen him die. We were so absorbed that we hardly noticed that a man had come alongside and was walking with us.

He courteously asked us what we were talking about, and, since he seemed very interested, we poured out the whole story of our shattered hopes. He quietly listened to it all. I suppose we covered two miles giving him just the bare facts.

Then he started to talk. First of all, he called us foolish and slow of heart to believe the prophets. And then he carefully explained to us that what had happened to our Christ was in full accord with the words of Moses and Isaiah and the other prophets. It was the best explanation of the scriptures Mary and I had ever experienced.

He seemed to put it all together for us. Jesus' death was God's way of taking care of humanity's sin problem. His resurrection was God's stamp of approval on the value of that death. That resurrection declared beyond any doubt that Jesus was the way, the truth, and the life, and that no one could come unto the father but through him.

As he talked, the last miles of our trip vanished like some kind of magic. Soon we were drawing near our village of Emmaus. A few more minutes and we were at our door. The friendly stranger waved a goodbye and started on his way.

I looked at Mary. We have been married for many years, and I have learned not to invite guests without checking. But Mary anticipated my wish and nodded vigorously. "Hurry," she whispered urgently.

I suddenly realized that I didn't know the man's name, but I called after him, "Friend, brother, abide with us, for it is eventide, and the day is far spent."

He paused, and smiled, and accepted our invitation. And I was haunted as I had been a number of times during the past miles with the feeling that this stranger was somehow familiar. He came into our home and we sat down while Mary got supper ready. Each of us was occupied with his own thoughts. There was an awful lot to think about. I was even daring to think some bold new ideas. Could Jesus possibly be alive as the stranger affirmed? I was just ready to ask him a question about this, but Mary called us to the table.

After we were seated I picked up a loaf of bread to bless it, as is our tradition. But this didn't seem proper even though I was the host. Mary was a bit surprised when I handed the bread to our guest and asked him to say the blessing.

He took the bread in his hands and prayed a prayer of blessing which included some words about the bread of life. He prayed clearly and firmly like one with authority, not the way our scribes drone on. When he finished his prayer he broke bread and handed a piece to Mary, and that was really different. Men are always served first, you know. But somehow I didn't mind.

And then Mary gasped. I looked at her and she was staring transfixed at his hands. So I looked too. There were nail prints! It was the Lord himself! Mary turned as pale as death, and I jumped to my feet so quickly that my bench crashed to the floor. And at that moment he vanished. He was gone. Mary and I had entertained the resurrected *Lord* at our own table! Our ***Christ*** was alive! Our Christ was *alive!*

We forgot all about eating! And we exclaimed to each other, "Didn't our hearts burn within us while he talked to us on the road, while he opened to us the Scriptures? We should have known! We *were* fools and slow of heart as he had said on the way."

I grabbed my wife by her hands and danced her around the kitchen! We were young and in love again—in love with the Messiah who made us forever young by his victory over death and the grave! Nothing we could do in celebration could be foolish!

As Mary and I were revelling in our new-found hope of a living Saviour and eternal life, I suddenly thought of the four lepers outside the besieged city of Samaria. They discovered lifegiving food while the people inside were so starved they were eating their babies. And the lepers said, "We do not well, this is a day of good tidings, and we hold our peace." And they promptly carried the good news to the suffering people.

But even before I could say anything, Mary declared, "Cleopas, we must go back to Jerusalem! We must tell the others that Jesus is alive and that we saw him and talked to him!"

I looked at the food on the table. Mary was a good housekeeper and never in all our years together would she set out on a trip without having everything in order. So, although I wanted to rush out of the house that very moment, I was resigned to the inevitable delay.

But she surprised me. "Who cares about bread drying out and bowls getting stained when our Lord who was dead is alive again?" In that moment of breathless excitement she was more beautiful than I had ever known her to be. She seemed to have been born again.

We burst out of our house like a couple of school children just dismissed by the Rabbi at the synagogue. We felt a bit foolish when some neighbors saw us going. But we didn't care. Jesus was alive! And we were more alive than ever before. We covered those seven miles with steps of joy, setting some kind of a new record for a no-longer-young husband and wife.

The trip home had been hopelessly long. The trip back to our Holy City was shortened by hope, and peace, and joy, and love. Jesus was ALIVE! Death couldn't hold him, or us, any more than a leaf could stop the Jordan River at flood-tide!

We hurried through the gate into Jerusalem, and panted through the streets to Mount Zion, where the Upper Room is. We climbed the steps and pounded on the locked door. When it was opened cautiously and we were let in, we were so out of breath that we just stood there and gasped. Before we could get a word out one of the disciples announced, "The Lord is risen. Simon has seen him."

We told our wonderful story! Mary usually lets me do the talking when men are present, but one week ago tonight she couldn't contain her joy. So we both related how the Lord had joined us and had sat at our table.

But somehow even then many in the room were incredulous. Thomas wondered how Mary and I could have spent a whole hour talking with Jesus and not recognize him. That was a good question. We were embarrassed. We had no reasonable answer.

Then suddenly everything got still. There was Jesus in our midst. The heavy door was still barred. His sudden appearance badly frightened us all. Many in our group were sure they were seeing a ghost. Seeing someone alive after you have seen him crucified takes some getting used to!

Then Jesus said, "Shalom, peace be unto you," just the way he had often done before. Then he said, "Why are you troubled? Behold my hands and my feet, that it is I myself. Handle me and see me, for a spirit has not flesh and bones as you see me have."

We just stood there all mixed up with joy and disbelief. Even Peter wasn't saying anything. A lot of old fears and ideas were being gently forced out of our minds by our loving Lord.

Then Jesus did a most understanding thing because he had also been human and therefore understood all about our doubts.

"Do you have anything for me to eat?" he asked quietly. And so Andrew gave him a piece of broiled fish, and one of the women offered him a honeycomb. And he ate them, Luke! Just stood there and ate everything. He was real and not a ghost, and he was alive!

Then we all sat down and he began to speak to us. Even though he repeated some things he had told Mary and me earlier that day, we didn't care.

He quoted sayings from the great prophet Isaiah. The ones I remember are:

"Therefore, the Lord himself shall give you a sign; Behold, a virgin shall conceive, and bear a son, and shall call his name Immanuel."

"Behold my servant, whom I uphold; mine elect, in whom my soul delighteth; I have put my spirit upon him; he shall bring forth judgment to the Gentiles."

"He was despised and rejected of men; a man of sorrows and acquainted with grief. We hid as it were our faces from him; he was despised, and we esteemed him not."

"Surely he hath borne our griefs, and carried our sorrows. Yet we did esteem him stricken, smitten of God, and afflicted. But he was wounded for our transgressions, he was bruised for our iniquities; the chastisement of our peace was upon him, and with his stripes we are healed. All we like sheep have gone astray; we have turned every one to his own way, and the Lord hath laid on him the iniquity of us all."

The Master then paused and slowly looked at us all. And we saw ourselves with deep pain as straying sheep, fleeing our Lord when he trudged his Via Dolorosa, his "sorrowful way."

Then he reminded us gently that "these are the words which I spake unto you, while I was yet with you, that all things must be fulfilled, which were written in the law of Moses, and in the prophets, and in the psalms, concerning me."

And then he opened our understanding. For the first time we clearly saw that the crucifixion was not just the cruel end of a hateful conspiracy, but the consummation of a glorious heavenly plan! He said, "Thus it is written, and thus it behooved me to suffer and to rise from the dead the third day."

Then the tone of his voice changed to one of firm command. "You shall preach the message of repentance and forgiveness of sins in my name to all nations of the world, beginning right here in Jerusalem. You are the witnesses of these things."

We all looked around at each other a bit sheepishly because we were at that very moment behind locked doors for fear of other Jews.

It had been around two hours after sunset when we arrived back at the upper room. Jesus appeared about an hour later and then spent two or three wonderful hours with us. Then, just as he had done in our home, he disappeared. Simply evaporated. But we had the serene feeling that somehow he was still with us, because he had just declared, "Lo, I am with you always, even unto the end of the world."

Well, Luke, that's the story. After staying in Jerusalem for the night, Mary and I came home the next morning. We have been telling everybody about our risen Lord, and some have come to believe fully in him. And they have become new people. When one comes to really believe that he will never die, life is forever changed.

One more thing. Mary and I have started a new tradition in our home. For a whole week we have set the place at the table where our Lord sat. That reminds us that he is always with us. Of course, he is right there in Antioch with you also, Luke, and with all the other believers everywhere.

Shalom,
Cleopas and Mary